hamlyn cookery club

Low-fat

pasta

hamlyn cookery club

Low-fat
pasta

First published in 2000 by Hamlyn
an imprint of Octopus Publishing Group Ltd
2–4 Heron Quays
London E14 4JP

British Library Cataloguing-in-Publication Data
A catalogue record for this book is available from the
British Library.

ISBN 0 600 60003 3

Printed in China

Copy Editor: Heather Thomas
Creative Director: Keith Martin
Design Manager: Bryan Dunn
Designer: Kevin Knight
Jacket Photography: Sean Myers
Picture Researcher: Christine Junemann
Senior Production Controller: Katherine Hockley

Notes

1 All the recipes in this book have been analysed by a professional nutritionist, so that you can see their nutritional content at a glance. The abbreviations are as follows: kcal = calories; kJ = kilojoules; CHO = carbohydrate. The analysis refers to each serving, unless otherwise stated, and does not include optional ingredients.

2 Both metric and imperial measurements have been given in all recipes. Use one set of measurements only and not a mixture of both.

3 Standard level spoon measurements are used in all recipes.
1 tablespoon = one 15 ml spoon
1 teaspoon = one 5 ml spoon

4 Eggs should be medium unless otherwise stated. The Department of Health advises that eggs should not be consumed raw. This book may contain dishes made with raw or lightly cooked eggs. It is prudent for more vulnerable people such as pregnant or nursing mothers, the elderly, babies and young children to avoid these dishes. Once prepared, these dishes should be refrigerated and eaten promptly.

5 Milk should be full fat unless otherwise stated.

6 Fresh herbs should be used unless otherwise stated. If unavailable use dried herbs as an alternative but halve the quantities stated.

7 Pepper should be freshly ground black pepper unless otherwise stated.

8 Ovens should be preheated to the specified temperature – if using a fan-assisted oven, follow the manufacturer's instructions for adjusting the time and temperature.

9 Measurements for canned food have been given as a standard metric equivalent.

10 Vegetarians should look for the 'V' symbol on a cheese to ensure it is made with vegetarian rennet.

Contents

Introduction

Tossed in a delicious low-fat sauce, pasta makes a nutritious, healthy meal. Pasta is the quintessential Italian food. Although it is low in fat, it is often served in creamy or oily high-fat sauces. In this inviting cookbook, however, you will find dozens of recipes for quick and easy low-fat pasta sauces.

WHAT IS PASTA?

Pasta can be bought fresh or dried. Dried pasta is made from flour and water – durum wheat flour is best as this helps cooked pasta to keep its bite and not to become soft and sticky. Sometimes eggs are added to the flour and water paste to enrich it. Fresh pasta is made from flour and eggs. Pasta also comes in many colours. For example, pasta may be coloured red with tomato purée, green with spinach or black with cuttlefish ink. Herbs and garlic can also be added to the pasta dough to add a distinctive flavour.

TYPES OF PASTA

Pasta comes in all shapes and sizes; in fact, there are over 300 varieties! You can choose from:
• Long pasta, such as spaghetti, linguine and capelli d'angelo (angel's hair pasta).
• Pasta ribbons, such as tagliatelle, fettuccine and pappardelle.
• Pasta tubes, such as macaroni, cannelloni and rigatoni.
• Short pasta, such as fusilli (spirals), conchiglie (shells) and penne (quills).

COOKING PASTA

To cook pasta successfully, you must bring a large saucepan of salted water to the boil. Ideally, you need approximately 1 litre (1¾ pints) water to every 125 g (4 oz) dried pasta. There is no need to add oil as long as you stir the pasta frequently while it is cooking. When the water comes to a rolling boil, add the pasta and bring back to boiling point. Boil, uncovered, stirring often, until the pasta is cooked. The time taken will depend on the type of pasta and whether it is fresh or dried. Fresh pasta cooks much more quickly. As a guideline, follow the manufacturer's instructions on the packet.

IS IT COOKED?

You can test whether the pasta is cooked by fishing out a piece or a strand and biting into it. It is cooked when it is *al dente* – slightly tender on the outside but it still has some bite. If it is still hard, leave it for another minute or two and test again. Never overcook pasta until it is soft and mushy. Drain in a large colander and always dress the hot pasta immediately with the sauce.

LOW-FAT PASTA SAUCES

Many traditional pasta sauces are made with lots of olive oil, butter or cream. However, you can cut down on fat by following these simple guidelines:

• Dry-fry the onion, garlic and vegetables in the sauce.

• Use a non-fat spray instead of oil or butter.

• Cook the vegetables in a little stock until tender instead of frying them.

• Don't mix cream or butter into a sauce at the end – use very low fat fromage frais or natural yogurt instead.

• Use low-fat lean meat, such as chicken, turkey and extra lean ground mince, rather than fatty meats, bacon and sausages. Always cut off and discard any fat before cooking.

• If using oily fish, such as sardines and salmon, use only small quantities in the sauce and bulk it out with extra vegetables.

• Don't add high- and medium-fat cheeses to pasta sauces – opt for low-fat ones.

• Don't toss the cooked pasta in olive oil or butter. Just toss lightly in a little of the cooked sauce and then pour the remaining sauce over the top.

SERVING PASTA

Always serve the cooked pasta on warm plates. It should never be served 'swimming' in its sauce. The sauce should cling to the pasta rather than lie in a pool around it. Parmesan cheese is the classic accompaniment but don't use too much as it is high in fat. It has a very strong flavour, so you need only a little – about 1 tablespoon of grated Parmesan should be sufficient to sprinkle over two to three servings of pasta. For the best flavour, grate a block of Parmesan rather than buying the ready-grated sort in little drums. Finally, provide your guests with a spoon as well as a knife and fork. This is useful for spooning up any delicious sauce or juices, and also for eating long pasta strands, such as spaghetti, which can be coiled around a fork resting in a spoon.

Meat Sauces

Chilli Chicken with Spinach Tagliolini

4 boneless, skinless chicken breasts, each about 75 g (3 oz)
1 teaspoon olive oil
2 green chillies, deseeded and sliced
1 green pepper, cored, deseeded and chopped
1 teaspoon lime juice

1 x 400 g (13 oz) can chopped tomatoes
15 g (½ oz) black olives, pitted
15 g (½ oz) green olives, pitted
250 g (8 oz) dried spinach tagliolini
salt and pepper
sprigs of flat leaf parsley, to garnish

Cut each chicken breast into 4 pieces. Heat the oil in a wok and add the chicken pieces, chillies and green pepper. Stir-fry for 5 minutes or until the chicken has browned.

Stir in the lime juice, tomatoes and olives, with salt and pepper to taste. Reduce the heat and simmer the sauce for 15 minutes.

Meanwhile, bring a large pan of salted water to the boil. Add the pasta, stir and cook for about 8 minutes, until *al dente*. Drain well, pile on to a large heated platter and spoon over the chicken mixture. Garnish with flat leaf parsley sprigs and serve immediately.

Serves 4

kcal 339; kJ 1423; protein 25 (g); fat 5 (g); CHO 49 (g)

Rigatoni with Chicken Livers and Herbs

250 g (8 oz) mushrooms, sliced
2–3 garlic cloves, crushed
1 tablespoon finely chopped thyme
1 tablespoon finely chopped sage
1 tablespoon olive oil
250 g (8 oz) chicken livers, trimmed
  and cut into small dice
4 tablespoons medium dry sherry
375 g (12 oz) dried rigatoni or
  penne
salt and pepper

Sauté the mushrooms, garlic and herbs in the oil in a pan for about 10 minutes, stirring frequently. Season with salt and pepper to taste. Remove the mushrooms with a slotted spoon and set aside.

Add the chicken livers and fry briskly over a high heat for about 5 minutes until tender but still pink and juicy in the centre.

Return the mushrooms to the pan with their juices and the sherry. Toss the ingredients together and adjust the seasoning if necessary.

Meanwhile, bring a large pan of salted water to the boil, add the rigatoni or penne, stir and bring back to the boil. Reduce the heat and boil, uncovered, for about 10 minutes or according to the packet instructions until *al dente*. Drain the pasta and transfer to a warm serving bowl. Pour over the chicken liver mixture and combine the pasta and sauce. Serve at once.

Serves 4

kcal 435; kJ 1846; protein 24 (g);
fat 6 (g); CHO 72 (g)

far left: chilli chicken with spinach tagliolini
below: rigatoni with chicken livers and herbs

Pasta with Chicken and Tomato Sauce

1 tablespoon olive oil

250 g (8 oz) boneless, skinless chicken breasts, diced

1 large onion, finely chopped

3 celery sticks, diced

2 carrots, diced

2 teaspoons dried oregano

125 ml (4 fl oz) red wine

425 g (14 oz) can chopped tomatoes

375 g (12 oz) conchiglie or penne

salt and pepper

Heat the oil and fry the chicken, stirring occasionally, until lightly coloured. Add the onion, celery and carrots and cook for 5 minutes until softened. Add the oregano, wine, tomatoes and seasoning. Bring to the boil, cover and simmer for 10 minutes.

Cook the pasta in boiling salted water for about 10 minutes until *al dente*. Drain and toss with half of the sauce. Transfer to a serving dish, spoon the remaining sauce over the top and serve immediately.

Serves 6

kcal 326; kJ 1383; protein 18 (g); fat 5 (g); CHO 54 (g)

Spaghetti alla Bolognese

500 g (1 lb) dried spaghetti

2 tablespoons vegetable stock

2 Spanish onions, chopped

1 tablespoon finely chopped rosemary

2 garlic cloves, crushed

2 x 425 g (14 oz) cans chopped tomatoes

5 tablespoons tomato purée

½ teaspoon sugar

250 g (8 oz) lean minced beef

salt and pepper

Bring a large saucepan of salted water to the boil. Add the spaghetti, stir and cook for about 8 minutes until *al dente*. Drain and season with pepper.

Meanwhile, heat the stock in a saucepan, add the onions and cook until softened. Add the rosemary and garlic and cook gently for 1 minute. Stir in the tomatoes, tomato purée, sugar and salt and pepper to taste. Simmer gently for 10–15 minutes.

Mix in the minced beef and stir until browned. Gently bring back to the boil and simmer for about 8 minutes, or until the meat is cooked and the sauce thickened. Pour over the spaghetti and serve at once.

Serves 4

kcal 588; kJ 2497; protein 32 (g);
fat 6 (g); CHO 109 (g)

Stir-fried Steak and Tagliatelle

1 garlic clove, crushed
1 teaspoon finely chopped fresh root
 ginger
25 g (1 oz) finely chopped onion
200 g (7 oz) lean steak, cut into thin
 4 cm (1½ inch) strips, fat removed
175 g (6 oz) broccoli florets, finely
 sliced
125 g (4 oz) mushrooms, finely
 sliced
2 tablespoons light soy sauce
4 tablespoons vegetable stock
1 teaspoon caster sugar
500 g (1 lb) dried tagliatelle
salt and pepper

Dry-fry the garlic, ginger, onion and a pinch of salt for 2–3 minutes, turning constantly, over a moderate heat. Add the steak and stir-fry for 2–3 minutes until brown all over.

Add the broccoli and stir-fry for 2 minutes. Add the mushrooms, soy sauce, stock and sugar and stir-fry for a further 3–4 minutes.

Meanwhile, bring a large pan of salted water to the boil. Add the pasta, stir and cook for 8 minutes, until *al dente*. Drain the pasta, add to the wok and toss for a few more minutes to allow the pasta to absorb some of the juices. Add freshly ground black pepper to taste. Serve immediately.

Serves 4

kcal 524; kJ 2194; protein 28 (g);
fat 4 (g); CHO 93 (g)

far left: spaghetti alla Bolognese
above: stir-fried steak and tagliatelle

Coriander and Chive Meatballs

Make sure you use extra lean minced beef to make these aromatic meatballs. They make a filling, robust meal as they are served with spaghetti and a tasty tomato sauce.

1 onion, grated
1 tablespoon freshly grated Parmesan cheese
150 g (5 oz) lean minced beef
1 tablespoon tomato purée
1 teaspoon chilli sauce

1 bunch coriander, finely chopped
1 bunch chives, chopped
125 g (4 oz) very finely chopped mushrooms
2 teaspoons sunflower oil
375 g (12 oz) dried spaghetti
salt and pepper
sprigs of basil, to garnish

Sauce:
1 onion, finely chopped
2 garlic cloves, crushed
425 g (14 oz) can chopped tomatoes with herbs
2 tablespoons tomato purée
2 tablespoons chopped oregano

To make the meatballs, combine the onion, Parmesan, minced beef, tomato purée, chilli sauce, herbs and mushrooms in a bowl. Season with salt and pepper and mix thoroughly.

Using dampened hands, shape the mixture into small balls. Heat the oil in a frying pan and then fry the meatballs, in batches, for 10 minutes until browned. Using a slotted spoon, transfer the meatballs to a baking dish. Keep warm.

Bring a large pan of salted water to the boil. Add the pasta, stir well and cook for about 8 minutes, or according to packet instructions, until *al dente*.

Meanwhile, make the sauce. Heat a frying pan, add the onion and garlic and dry-fry for 3–6 minutes, stirring constantly, until softened. Stir in the tomatoes, tomato purée and oregano. Simmer gently for 8 minutes, and then season to taste with salt and pepper.

Drain the pasta and pile it into a heated bowl. Pour over the tomato sauce and toss lightly together. Serve immediately with the meatballs, garnished with basil.

Serves 6

kcal 300; kJ 1276; protein 16 (g); fat 4 (g); CHO 53 (g)

left: coriander and chive meatballs
far right: pasta with peperoni, onion and balsamic vinegar sauce

Pasta with Peperoni, Onion and Balsamic Vinegar Sauce

1 teaspoon olive oil

3 large onions, thinly sliced into rings

75 g (3 oz) peperoni, sliced

300 ml (½ pint) vegetable stock

4 tablespoons chopped fresh flat leaf
  parsley

1 tablespoon balsamic vinegar

375 g (12 oz) conchiglie or gnocchi

salt and black pepper

Heat the oil in a large pan and cook
the onions gently over a low heat
for 40 minutes, until very soft and
slightly caramelized.

Raise the heat, add the peperoni
and stir-fry for a few minutes until
heated through. Pour in the stock
and bring to the boil, scraping up
any sediment from the bottom of
the pan. Stir in the parsley and
balsamic vinegar, and season to
taste with salt and pepper.

Cook the pasta in plenty of
boiling salted water for about 10
minutes until *al dente*. Drain, toss
with the sauce and serve
immediately.

Serves 6

kcal 335; kJ 1413; protein 12 (g);
fat 8 (g); CHO 57 (g)

Conchiglie with Calabrian Sauce

625 g (1¼ lb) canned tomatoes

non-fat spray, for spraying

2 garlic cloves, each cut into 3–4
  pieces

1 chilli

50 g (2 oz) Calabrese salami, thickly
  sliced

500 g (1 lb) dried conchiglie

15 g (½ oz) pecorino cheese, grated

salt

Prepare the sauce before cooking the pasta. Crush the tomatoes or blend them briefly in a liquidizer.

Spray a pan with non-fat spray, heat gently and add the garlic and chilli. Sauté until the garlic is golden, crushing the chilli against the pan to release its flavour.

Add the tomatoes and the slices of salami with salt to taste. Simmer gently for about 30 minutes until the sauce becomes denser and darker in colour.

Meanwhile, cook the conchiglie in boiling, salted water for about 10 minutes, or according to the packet instructions, until *al dente*. Drain, transfer to a serving dish and pour the sauce over the top. Serve with the grated pecorino.

Serves 4

kcal 537; kJ 2280; protein 20 (g);
fat 9 (g); CHO 100 (g)

Spaghetti with Casserole Sauce

To make the sauce more colourful and interesting, you could add some dry-fried onion and garlic. It can be served with any dried pasta.

250 g (8 oz) lean finely minced beef

250 g (8 oz) button mushrooms,
  quartered

4 tablespoons dry white wine

500 g (1 lb) dried spaghetti

25 g (1 oz) Parmesan cheese, grated

salt and pepper

Start making the sauce before cooking the spaghetti. In an earthenware casserole, dry-fry the minced beef gently, stirring thoroughly so that it does not stick together. Add the mushrooms and continue cooking until both the beef and mushrooms are cooked.

Add salt to taste and a generous quantity of pepper. Pour in the wine and cook gently until it evaporates.

Meanwhile, cook the spaghetti in plenty of boiling water for about 8 minutes until *al dente*. Drain and mix thoroughly with the sauce, adding half of the Parmesan. Serve with the remaining Parmesan.

Serves 4

kcal 550; kJ 2336; protein 31 (g);
fat 8 (g); CHO 93 (g)

Pasta with Red Sauce with Peas

125 g (4 oz) rindless lean smoked
  bacon, diced

125 g (4 oz) frozen peas

500 g (1 lb) plum tomatoes, skinned
  and chopped (or canned)

250 ml (8 fl oz) vegetable stock

375 g (12 oz) dried pasta of your
  choice

salt and pepper

Dry-fry the bacon in a small pan over a medium heat. Before it becomes crisp, add the peas and leave to flavour for 2 minutes.

Add the tomatoes to the pan, adjust the seasoning, pour in the stock and cook over a low heat for 30 minutes, stirring from time to time to prevent the sauce from sticking to the pan. Season to taste with salt and pepper before serving.

Meanwhile, cook the pasta of your choice in plenty of boiling salted water for about 8–10 minutes, or according to the packet instructions, until *al dente*. Drain and toss with the sauce. Serve immediately.

Serves 4

kcal 335; kJ 1423; protein 25 (g);
fat 5 (g); CHO 50 (g)

right: spaghetti with casserole sauce (top); conchiglie with Calabrian sauce (bottom)

Tagliatelle with Ham, Pea and Mushroom Sauce

250 g (8 oz) mushrooms, thinly sliced
3–4 tablespoons vegetable stock
125 g (4 oz) frozen peas
125 g (4 oz) lean cooked ham, cut
   into matchstick strips
300 ml (½ pint) very low-fat natural
   fromage frais
50 g (2 oz) grated Parmesan cheese
500 g (1 lb) tagliatelle or fettuccine
salt and pepper

Gently cook the mushrooms in the stock until just tender. Season to taste with salt and pepper. Cook the peas in boiling salted water (see packet instructions) and drain.

Add the peas and ham to the mushrooms with their juice, and stir in the fromage frais. Add half of the grated Parmesan and heat through very gently over a low heat without boiling.

Cook the pasta in boiling salted water for about 8 minutes until *al dente*. Drain and toss with half of the sauce. Transfer to a serving dish and then spoon the rest of the sauce over the top. Serve with the remaining Parmesan.

Serves 6

kcal 396; kJ 1662; protein 23 (g);
fat 5 (g); CHO 66 (g)

Ribbon Noodles with Herbs and Bacon

You can vary the herbs in this recipe according to the time of year and which herbs are in season. We have used basil, a pungent summery herb, with parsley, but you could try chives or oregano.

1 tablespoon olive oil
125 g (4 oz) lean bacon lardons
1 onion, chopped
150 ml (¼ pint) chicken stock
1 tablespoon chopped parsley
4 basil leaves, chopped
425 g (14 oz) dried fettuccine
25 g (1 oz) pecorino cheese, grated
salt and pepper

Heat the oil in a heavy pan, add the bacon and onion and cook gently for 5 minutes. Add the stock, parsley, basil and salt and pepper to taste. Simmer gently, stirring occasionally, until reduced and slightly thickened.

Meanwhile, cook the fettuccine in plenty of boiling, salted water for about 8 minutes until *al dente*. Drain thoroughly and pile into a warmed serving dish. Add the sauce and pecorino and fold gently to mix. Serve immediately.

Serves 4

kcal 477; kJ 2019; protein 22 (g);
fat 9 (g); CHO 82 (g)

Green Noodles with Blue Cheese

375 g (12 oz) dried green spinach
   noodles
75 g (3 oz) rindless lean bacon,
   chopped
250 g (8 oz) cottage cheese
50 g (2 oz) Roquefort cheese,
   crumbled
2 spring onions, thinly sliced
salt and pepper

Cook the noodles in plenty of boiling, salted water for about 8 minutes, or according to the packet instructions, until *al dente*. Drain the noodles, refresh in hot water and drain again.

Meanwhile, cook the bacon over a moderate heat until the fat has run and the bacon is crispy. Remove with a slotted spoon and reserve.

Toss the noodles with the cheeses and spring onions and season to taste with salt and pepper. Stir in the cooked bacon. Transfer the noodles to a heated serving dish and serve immediately.

Serves 4

kcal 460; kJ 1930; protein 26 (g);
fat 9 (g); CHO 69 (g)

far left: tagliatelle with ham, pea and mushroom sauce

Tagliatelle Romana

1.5 litres (2½ pints) chicken stock
250 g (8 oz) dried tagliatelle
125 g (4 oz) Quark cheese
1 garlic clove, crushed
50 g (2 oz) smoked prosciutto, fat
   removed and cut into strips
salt and pepper
finely chopped oregano, to garnish

Put the chicken stock in a large saucepan and bring to the boil. Add the tagliatelle, stir and cook for about 8 minutes, or according to the packet instructions, until *al dente*, then drain and transfer to a hot serving dish.

Sieve the Quark and mix in the garlic. Season with salt and pepper. Stir the cheese mixture into the tagliatelle and then toss with the strips of prosciutto. Garnish with chopped oregano and serve immediately.

Serves 4

kcal 267; kJ 1119; protein 16 (g);
fat 2 (g); CHO 46 (g)

left: tagliatelle Romana
right: tagliatelle Riviera

Tagliatelle Riviera

A delicious accompaniment to this pasta dish is a fresh rocket and basil salad lightly tossed with a low-fat vinaigrette dressing.

2 teaspoons olive oil

2 onions, sliced

2 garlic cloves, crushed

2 rashers lean back bacon, fat removed, derinded and chopped

250 g (8 oz) mushrooms, sliced

2 anchovy fillets, chopped

6 black olives, pitted and halved

500 g (1 lb) dried tagliatelle

salt and pepper

1 tablespoon freshly grated Parmesan cheese, to serve

basil leaves, to garnish

Heat the oil and fry the onions, garlic and bacon until the onions are soft but not brown. Stir in the mushrooms, anchovy fillets, olives and salt and pepper to taste. Cook for a further 4–5 minutes.

Meanwhile, bring a large pan of salted water to the boil. Add the pasta, stir and cook for about 8 minutes, or according to the packet instructions, until *al dente*. Drain the tagliatelle and arrange in a warm bowl. To serve, spoon over the sauce and sprinkle with grated Parmesan and fresh basil leaves.

Serves 4

kcal 518; kJ 2167; protein 20 (g); fat 6 (g); CHO 97 (g)

Fusilli with Peperoni Sauce

1 teaspoon olive oil

2 red peppers, cored, deseeded and cut into thin strips

10 black olives, pitted and chopped

1 tablespoon capers

75 g (3 oz) peperoni, thinly sliced

500 g (1 lb) dried fusilli

50 g (2 oz) Parmesan cheese, grated

drop of milk

salt and pepper

Heat the olive oil and gently fry the peppers until tender, adding the olives and capers halfway through the cooking time. Add the peperoni. Season to taste, then strain off the excess olive oil.

Meanwhile, cook the fusilli in plenty of boiling, salted water for about 10 minutes, until *al dente*. Drain, transfer to a serving dish and pour the sauce over the top. Add the Parmesan and milk and mix thoroughly. Add a little more milk if necessary to form a moist, creamy mixture. Spoon over the sauce and serve immediately.

Serves 4

kcal 490; kJ 2077; protein 19 (g); fat 9 (g); CHO 89 (g)

Macaroni with Ham, Tomato and Cheese Sauce

2 teaspoons olive oil

3 garlic cloves, finely chopped

175 g (6 oz) cooked lean ham, finely diced

425 g (14 oz) can chopped plum tomatoes

500 g (1 lb) dried macaroni

2 tablespoons chopped fresh basil

50 g (2 oz) freshly grated pecorino or Parmesan cheese

salt and pepper

Heat the oil over a medium heat. Add the garlic and ham, and gently sauté for 4–5 minutes. Add the tomatoes, and salt and pepper to taste. Simmer gently for 10–15 minutes until well blended, stirring frequently.

Cook the macaroni in plenty of boiling salted water for about 8 minutes until *al dente*. Drain and toss with half of the sauce. Transfer to a serving dish and spoon the remaining sauce over the top. Mix the basil with the grated cheese and sprinkle over the macaroni. Serve immediately.

Serves 6

kcal 380; kJ 1615; protein 20 (g); fat 6 (g); CHO 66 (g)

Penne with Mushroom, Bacon and Tomato Sauce

Robust tubular pasta, such as macaroni or penne, are perfect with this colourful sauce. However, you could substitute any other dried pasta shapes, if liked.

1 teaspoon oil

125 g (4 oz) lean back bacon, derinded and diced

375 g (12 oz) mushrooms, sliced

2 garlic cloves, sliced

½ fresh chilli, deseeded and chopped

500 g (1 lb) tomatoes, skinned and chopped

fresh basil leaves, torn

500 g (1 lb) dried penne or macaroni

50 g (2 oz) freshly grated Parmesan or pecorino cheese

salt

Heat the oil in a frying pan, add the bacon and gently fry until lightly browned. Remove the bacon from the pan with a slotted spoon and drain on kitchen paper.

Add the mushrooms to the pan and cook gently until softened and lightly browned. Remove them with a slotted spoon and then set aside.

Sauté the garlic and chilli in the same pan. When the garlic is golden brown, discard it together with the chilli. Add the tomatoes to the pan

with the basil. Season to taste with salt and simmer for 20 minutes.

Stir in the bacon and mushrooms, and simmer gently over a low heat for a few more minutes.

Meanwhile, cook the pasta in plenty of boiling salted water for about 10 minutes, or according to the packet instructions, until *al dente*. Drain and transfer to a heated serving dish. Toss with the grated Parmesan or pecorino and pour the sauce over the top. Toss gently together and serve immediately.

Serves 6

kcal 386; kJ 1640; protein 19 (g); fat 7 (g); CHO 66 (g)

---

above: *penne with mushroom, bacon and tomato sauce*

Bucatini with Amatrice Sauce

2 teaspoons olive oil
1 chilli
1 onion, finely chopped
75 g (3 oz) rindless lean bacon, cut
    into 1 cm (½ inch) squares
1 tablespoon tomato purée
2 x 425 g (14 oz) cans tomatoes,
    crushed or blended
500 g (1 lb) dried bucatini
25 g (1 oz) pecorino cheese, grated
salt and pepper

Start making the sauce before cooking the pasta. Heat the oil in a large frying pan and add the chilli and onion. Fry the onion gently until transparent and crush the chilli against the bottom of the pan to release its flavour.

Add the bacon and then fry until crispy, stirring all the time. Add the tomato purée and the tomatoes with some salt and pepper to taste. Simmer gently for about 30 minutes until the sauce becomes denser and darker in colour.

Meanwhile, cook the bucatini in plenty of boiling, salted water for about 8 minutes, or according to the packet instructions, until *al dente*, then drain. Put half of the cheese in a serving dish, add the freshly cooked pasta and pour the sauce over the pasta while mixing it with the remaining cheese. Serve immediately.

Serves 4

kcal 547; kJ 2523; protein 24 (g); fat 8 (g); CHO 103 (g)

Cook's Tip: Bucatini is a thick spaghetti with a hole through the centre. It originated in Rome where it is often served with this sauce.

Fettuccine with Prosciutto, Chilli and Tomato Sauce

Any broad or narrow ribbon pasta or even spaghetti or linguine can be used in this recipe.

2 teaspoons olive oil
1 onion, finely chopped
125 g (4 oz) lean prosciutto, diced
2 garlic cloves, crushed
1 fresh chilli, deseeded and finely chopped
750 g (1½ lb) tomatoes, skinned and chopped
salt and freshly ground black pepper
500 g (1 lb) fettuccine or tagliatelle
25 g (1 oz) freshly grated pecorino cheese

Heat the oil in a large frying pan and gently fry the onion for about 3 minutes until translucent and softened but not browned.

Add the prosciutto and cook for a further 2–3 minutes. Stir in the garlic, chilli and tomatoes, and season to taste. Cook gently for 10 minutes until the sauce thickens.

Cook the pasta in plenty of boiling salted water for about 8 minutes, or according to the packet instructions, until *al dente*. Drain well and toss with the sauce and grated pecorino. Transfer to a heated serving dish and serve immediately.

Serves 6

kcal 395; kJ 1652; protein 19 (g); fat 6 (g); CHO 66 (g)

far left: bucatini with amatrice sauce
above: fettuccine with prosciutto, chilli and tomato sauce

Macaroni with Sausage and Tomato Sauce

1 teaspoon olive oil

1 large onion, chopped

2 garlic cloves, crushed

125 g (4 oz) Italian sausages, skinned and coarsely chopped

1 red pepper, cored, deseeded and cut into 1 cm (½ inch) squares

750 g (1½ lb) tomatoes, skinned and chopped

2 teaspoons dried oregano

2 tablespoons tomato purée

250 g (8 oz) dried macaroni or rigatoni

salt and pepper

Heat the oil in a pan and gently fry the onion until soft. Add the garlic and fry until beginning to colour. Add the sausage to the pan and fry until evenly browned.

Add the red pepper, tomatoes, oregano and tomato purée, and then season to taste with salt and pepper. Cook gently, uncovered, for 12–15 minutes.

Cook the pasta in plenty of boiling salted water for about 8 minutes, or according to the packet instructions, until *al dente*. Drain well and toss with the sauce. Transfer to a warm serving dish and serve immediately.

Serves 4

kcal 375; kJ 1587; protein 15 (g); fat 9 (g); CHO 62 (g)

below: *macaroni with sausage and tomato sauce*

Pasta al Funghi

375 g (12 oz) dried pasta of your
  choice
non-fat spray, for spraying
500 g (1 lb) fresh mushrooms, sliced
75 g (3 oz) lean bacon cubes
125 g (4 oz) dried ceps or chanterelles,
  soaked for 15 minutes and drained
pinch of grated nutmeg
150 g (5 oz) very low-fat natural
  fromage frais
2 tablespoons finely chopped parsley
1 level tablespoon grated Parmesan
  cheese
salt and pepper

Cook the pasta in a large pan of
boiling lightly salted water for
about 8–10 minutes, until *al dente*.
Drain well in a colander.

While the pasta is cooking, spray
a large frying pan with non-fat
spray and heat gently. Add the
sliced mushrooms and bacon and
cook for about 5 minutes until
golden brown. Stir in the drained,
soaked mushrooms and nutmeg.

Gently fold in the fromage frais
over a very low heat and heat
through gently. Season to taste with
salt and pepper. Tip the drained
pasta into the pan and toss gently
to coat it evenly with the sauce.
Sprinkle with parsley and Parmesan,
and serve immediately.

Serves 4

kcal 490; kJ 2079; protein 24 (g);
fat 5 (g); CHO 93 (g)

Country-style Macaroni

2 anchovy fillets, soaked in a little
  milk
1 teaspoon olive oil
1 garlic clove, unpeeled
50 g (2 oz) rindless lean bacon
  lardons
425 g (14 oz) can plum tomatoes
50 g (2 oz) pitted black olives,
  chopped
¼ teaspoon chopped oregano
375 g (12 oz) dried macaroni
25 g (1 oz) pecorino cheese, grated
salt and pepper

Drain the anchovies. Heat the oil in
a small pan and add the garlic and
anchovies. Cook over a medium
heat for a few minutes, and then
remove the garlic and add the
bacon. Add the tomatoes to the pan
when the bacon is crisp.

Season with salt and pepper and
cook over a low heat for about
20 minutes until the sauce thickens.
Add the olives and oregano halfway
through the cooking time.

Cook the pasta in plenty of
boiling salted water for about
8 minutes until *al dente*. Drain,
transfer to a heated serving dish,
pour the sauce over the top and
sprinkle with pecorino cheese.

Serves 4

kcal 414; kJ 1758; protein 18 (g);
fat 7 (g); CHO 74 (g)

Penne with Chilli Sauce

1 teaspoon olive oil
1 large onion, finely chopped
2 garlic cloves, crushed
125 g (4 oz) rindless lean bacon,
  chopped
1–2 fresh red chillies, deseeded and
  chopped
425 g (14 oz) can chopped tomatoes
25 g (1 oz) pecorino or Parmesan
  cheese, grated
500 g (1 lb) dried penne
salt and pepper

Heat the oil in a pan and cook the
onion, garlic and bacon until they
are lightly coloured. Add the chillies,
tomatoes and most of the cheese.
Season to taste with salt and pepper
and cook over a gentle heat for
30–40 minutes until the sauce
thickens. Check the seasoning.

Cook the penne in boiling salted
water for about 10 minutes, or
according to the packet instructions,
until *al dente*. Drain well and place
in a hot serving dish. Stir in most of
the sauce, then pour the remaining
sauce over the top. Serve the rest of
the cheese separately.

Serves 4

kcal 555; kJ 2359; protein 26 (g);
fat 8 (g); CHO 103 (g)

Vegetarian Sauces

Fusilli with Aubergine and Tomato Sauce

1 large aubergine, diced
non-fat spray, for spraying
500 g (1 lb) dried fusilli
1 quantity Tomato and Garlic Sauce
    (see right)
salt and pepper
basil leaves or sprigs of parsley, to
    garnish

Spread the diced aubergine on a wire cooking rack over a tray and sprinkle over 1–2 teaspoons salt. Leave for at least 30 minutes to drain. This will remove some of the liquid and the bitter flavour from the aubergine. Rinse thoroughly, drain well and pat dry on kitchen paper.

Spray a frying pan with non-fat spray and place over a low heat. Add some of the aubergine and then cook gently, stirring, until golden brown all over. Repeat until all the aubergine dice are cooked. Keep hot.

Cook the fusilli in boiling salted water for about 10 minutes until *al dente*. Drain well and stir into the hot tomato sauce. Check the seasoning and add salt and pepper to taste.

Pour into a serving bowl and then arrange the fried aubergine on top. Sprinkle with the chopped basil or parsley just before serving.

Serves 4

kcal 519; kJ 2206; protein 19 (g);
fat 4 (g); CHO 109 (g)

Tagliatelle with Tomato Sauce

non-fat spray, for spraying
2 onions, chopped
2 garlic cloves, crushed
500 g (1 lb) plum tomatoes, skinned
    and chopped
2 tablespoons tomato purée
1 teaspoon sugar
125 ml (4 fl oz) dry white wine
ripe olives, pitted and quartered
a handful of torn basil leaves
250 g (8 oz) dried tagliatelle
salt and pepper

Spray a large frying pan with non-fat spray and place over a low heat. Add the onions and garlic and sauté gently until they are tender and slightly coloured. Stir the mixture occasionally.

Add the tomatoes, tomato purée, sugar and wine, stirring well. Cook over a gentle heat until the mixture is quite thick and reduced. Stir in the olives and basil leaves and then season to taste with salt and plenty of black pepper.

Meanwhile, add the tagliatelle to a large pan of boiling salted water, stir and cook for about 8 minutes until *al dente*. Drain the tagliatelle and add a generous grinding of black pepper.

Arrange the pasta on 4 serving plates and top with the tomato sauce, mixing it gently into the tagliatelle. Serve at once.

Serves 6

kcal 190; kJ 797; protein 6 (g);
fat 1 (g); CHO 36 (g)

Linguine with Tomato and Garlic Sauce

500 g (1 lb) dried inguine
Tomato and Garlic Sauce:
1 tablespoon olive oil
1 kg (2 lb) plum tomatoes, skinned
    and chopped
4 garlic cloves, finely chopped
½ teaspoon dried oregano
1 tablespoon chopped parsley
salt and pepper
freshly grated Parmesan cheese, to
    serve

Heat the oil in a pan and gently fry the tomatoes and garlic over a medium-high heat for 20 minutes until thickened. Add the oregano, parsley and salt and pepper to taste, and cook for a few minutes.

Meanwhile, cook the pasta in plenty of boiling salted water for about 8 minutes, or according to the packet instrcutions, until *al dente*. Drain well and mix with the sauce. Transfer to a heated dish and serve with the grated Parmesan.

above: fusilli with aubergine and tomato sauce

Serves 6

kcal 340; kJ 1447; protein 12 (g); fat 5 (g); CHO 67 (g)

Fettuccine with Courgette and Rosemary Sauce

This makes a lovely summer dish when courgettes are plentiful. The rosemary adds a distinctive flavour to the sauce. For a more creamy sauce, you could stir in a little very low-fat natural fromage frais just before serving the pasta.

500 g (1 lb) courgettes, cut into matchstick strips
1 tablespoon olive oil
2 onions, very thinly sliced
1 garlic clove, finely chopped
1 tablespoon finely chopped flat leaf parsley
2 tablespoons finely chopped rosemary
500 g (1 lb) fresh fettuccine
25 g (1 oz) freshly grated Parmesan cheese
salt and pepper

Put the courgettes in a colander, sprinkle with salt and then leave to drain for 1 hour. Pat dry with some kitchen paper.

Heat the oil and gently fry the onions until golden. Add the garlic, parsley and courgettes, and cook until just tender, stirring frequently. Stir in the rosemary and season to taste with salt and pepper.

Meanwhile, cook the pasta in plenty of boiling salted water for 3–4 minutes, or according to the packet instructions, until *al dente*. Drain and toss with half of the Parmesan and half of the sauce. Transfer to a serving dish and spoon the remaining sauce over the top. Sprinkle with the remaining Parmesan and serve immediately.

Serves 6

kcal 335; kJ 1340; protein 14 (g); fat 6 (g); CHO 58 (g)

Spaghetti with Fresh Tomato Sauce

This classic pasta dish is eaten widely throughout southern Italy. To reduce the fat content, we have omitted the usual olive oil and used a non-fat spray instead for cooking the vegetables.

non-fat spray, for spraying
2 celery sticks, finely chopped
1 large carrot, finely chopped
1 small onion, finely chopped
2 garlic cloves, crushed
1 kg (2 lb) ripe plum tomatoes, roughly chopped
1 teaspoon caster sugar
2 tablespoons chopped fresh basil
500 g (1 lb) spaghetti or linguine
salt and pepper
torn basil leaves, to garnish
freshly grated Parmesan cheese, to serve

Spray a pan with non-fat spray and place over a low heat. When hot, add the celery, carrot, onion and garlic and fry gently for 5 minutes until tender.

Stir in the tomatoes, sugar and basil, and season to taste with salt and pepper. Bring to the boil, then reduce the heat, cover the pan and simmer gently for 30 minutes. Transfer to a food processor or blender and purée the sauce. Rub the purée through a sieve.

Meanwhile, cook the pasta in plenty of boiling salted water for about 8 minutes until *al dente*. Drain and toss with the sauce. Transfer to a serving dish, garnish with basil, and serve immediately with Parmesan.

Serves 4

kcal 507; kJ 2159; protein 19 (g); fat 5 (g); CHO 104 (g)

Tomato and Red Wine Pasta

non-fat spray, for spraying
1 onion, finely chopped
2 garlic cloves, crushed
250 ml (8 fl oz) red wine
500 g (1 lb) plum tomatoes, skinned and chopped
1 tablespoon chopped parsley
1 tablespoon chopped basil
375 g (12 oz) dried pasta of your choice
salt and pepper

Spray a heavy shallow pan with non-fat spray and place over a low heat. Add the onion and garlic and cook gently for 5 minutes until translucent and softened.

Add the wine and leave on the low heat for 5 minutes to evaporate.

Add the tomatoes to the pan, season with salt and pepper and simmer gently for 20 minutes, stirring from time to time to prevent the sauce from sticking to the pan. Add the parsley and basil just before turning off the heat.

Meanwhile, cook the pasta in plenty of boiling salted water for about 8–10 minutes until *al dente*. Drain well and toss with the sauce. Serve at once.

Serves 4

kcal 399; kJ 1694; protein 13 (g); fat 2 (g); CHO 77 (g)

far left: fettuccine with courgette and rosemary sauce
below: tomato and red wine pasta

Penne with Uncooked Tomato and Basil sauce

500 g (1 lb) ripe plum tomatoes, skinned
4 teaspoons olive oil
1 garlic clove, crushed
bunch of fresh basil
375 g (12 oz) dried penne, conchiglie or farfalle
salt

Put the tomatoes either in a food processor or a blender and then purée them briefly. Add the olive oil and crushed garlic.

Wash and dry the basil leaves, discarding the stalks. Tear the leaves into small pieces and add to the tomato sauce. Leave the sauce to stand for about 30 minutes, then add salt to taste and stir well.

Bring a large saucepan of salted water to the boil. Add the pasta, stir and cook for about 10 minutes, or according to the packet instructions, until *al dente*. Drain and transfer to a warm serving dish. Pour the sauce over the top and serve immediately.

Serves 4

kcal 375: kJ 1596; protein 12 (g); fat 5 (g); CHO 75 (g)

Paglia e Fieno with Tomato and Rosemary

Whole dried chillies taste very hot so it is best to remove them from the sauce before serving.

625 g (1¼ lb) can plum tomatoes
1 tablespoon olive oil
1 small carrot, finely chopped
1 small onion, finely chopped
1 celery stick, finely chopped
about 4 tablespoons red wine
2 whole dried red chillies
250–300 g (8–10 oz) fresh plain paglia e fieno pasta, coiled into nests
2 teaspoons chopped rosemary
salt and pepper
sprigs of rosemary, to garnish

Purée the canned tomatoes and their juice in either a food processor or a blender.

Heat the oil in a heavy saucepan. Add the carrot, onion and celery and cook gently, stirring frequently, for 15 minutes or until soft. Add the red wine, increase the heat and then simmer until all the wine has been absorbed by the vegetables.

Add the puréed tomatoes and the whole chillies, then season to taste and bring to the boil. Reduce the heat, cover the pan and simmer for 15–20 minutes until the sauce is quite thick.

Meanwhile, bring a large pan of salted water to the boil. Add the pasta, stir and cook for 3–4 minutes until *al dente*. Drain the pasta and turn it into a warm bowl.

Remove the sauce from the heat and stir in the chopped rosemary. Check the seasoning and pour the hot sauce over the pasta. Serve garnished with rosemary sprigs.

Serves 4

kcal 302; kJ 1215; protein 11 (g); fat 5 (g); CHO 52 (g)

Pasta al Pomodoro

1 tablespoon olive oil
2 celery sticks, finely chopped
1 large carrot, finely chopped
1 small onion, finely chopped
2 garlic cloves, crushed
1 kg (2 lb) ripe plum tomatoes, roughly chopped
1 teaspoon caster sugar
2 tablespoons chopped basil
500 g (1 lb) dried spaghetti or linguine
salt and pepper
torn basil leaves, to garnish
freshly grated Parmesan cheese, to serve

Heat the oil in a saucepan, add the celery, carrot, onion and garlic and fry gently for 5 minutes until softened. Stir in the tomatoes, sugar and basil,

and season to taste with salt and pepper. Bring to the boil, cover and simmer gently for 30 minutes.

Transfer to a food processor or a blender and purée the sauce. Rub through a sieve and keep warm.

Bring a large saucepan of salted water to the boil. Add the pasta, stir and cook for about 8 minutes until *al dente*. Drain and toss with the sauce. Transfer to a serving dish, garnish with torn basil leaves and serve immediately with a little Parmesan.

Serves 4

kcal 510; kJ 2168; protein 17 (g); fat 6 (g); CHO 104 (g)

above: paglia e fieno with tomato and rosemary

Penne with Aubergine

Be adventurous in selecting pasta shapes. There is such a wide variety for you to experiment with. For instance, instead of using penne, try rigatoni or mezze maniche (short sleeves) which are other short, tubular types of pasta.

500 g (1 lb) aubergine, cubed
250 g (8 oz) dried penne
1 onion, chopped
2 garlic cloves, crushed
1 teaspoon mustard powder
1 tablespoon tomato purée
425 g (14 oz) can tomatoes
½ teaspoon oregano
1 tablespoon chopped parsley
salt and pepper

Put the aubergine in a colander and sprinkle with salt. Leave for 30 minutes to remove any bitter taste, then rinse well and pat dry with kitchen paper.

Bring a large saucepan of salted water to the boil. Add the pasta, stir and cook for about 10 minutes, or according to the packet instructions, until *al dente*. Drain and keep warm.

Meanwhile, simmer the onion and garlic in a little water for 3–6 minutes, stirring constantly. Transfer to a shallow baking dish and cook in a preheated oven, 180°C (350°F), Gas Mark 4, for about 6 minutes until softened. Return to a saucepan.

Add the aubergine to the pan and cook, stirring, until it is lightly browned. Stir in the mustard, tomato purée, tomatoes and their juice, herbs and pepper to taste. Simmer gently for 10 minutes over a low heat until the aubergine is cooked, stirring occasionally. Pour the hot sauce over the pasta and serve at once.

Serves 4

Kcal 275; kJ 1170; protein 11 (g); fat 2 (g); CHO 57 (g)

Farfalle with Tomatoes and Mushrooms

This simple dish is ideal for children who will enjoy it even more if it is made with tri-coloured pasta – plain, spinach- and tomato-flavoured.

175 g (6 oz) dried farfalle
salt and pepper
Sauce:
1 teaspoon sunflower oil
1 small onion, finely chopped
125 g (4 oz) mushrooms, sliced
425g (14 oz) can tomatoes
1 tablespoon chopped basil (optional)
salt and pepper

Bring a large pan of salted water to the boil. Add the pasta, then stir and cook for about 8 minutes, or according to the packet instructions, until *al dente*. Drain and keep warm.

Meanwhile, make the sauce. Heat the oil in a saucepan, add the onion and mushrooms and sauté for 5 minutes. Stir in the tomatoes and cook gently, uncovered, for 15 minutes to reduce the sauce. Add the basil, if using, and simmer for a further 5 minutes. Season to taste, pour over the pasta bows and serve.

Serves 2

kcal 364; kJ 1548; protein 14 (g); fat 4 (g); CHO 74 (g)

far left: penne with aubergine
below: *farfalle with tomatoes and mushrooms*

Spaghetti with Ratatouille Sauce

1 large onion, chopped
1 garlic clove, crushed
500 g (1 lb) courgettes, sliced
1 large aubergine, diced
1 green pepper, cored, deseeded and diced
500 g (1 lb) tomatoes, skinned and chopped
1 tablespoon chopped oregano or basil
500 g (1 lb) dried low-fat spaghetti
salt and pepper
1 tablespoon chopped parsley, to garnish

Put all the ingredients, except the pasta and parsley, into a large pan. Add enough water to cover the vegetables and cook gently, stirring occasionally, for 30 minutes until the vegetables are tender and the juices have thickened slightly.

Meanwhile, bring a large pan of salted water to the boil. Add the pasta, stir and cook for about 8 minutes until just *al dente*. Drain and place in a warmed serving dish.

Taste the sauce and adjust the seasoning. Pour over the pasta and serve, sprinkled with parsley.

Serves 4

kcal 522; kJ 2220; protein 20 (g); fat 4 (g); CHO 110 (g)

Bucatini del Buongustaio

Bucatini is a long thin pasta, not unlike spaghetti, which could be substituted if you prefer.

1 tablespoon olive oil
1 large onion, finely chopped
2 garlic cloves, finely chopped
1 aubergine, peeled and diced
125 g (4 oz) mushrooms, sliced
425 g (14 oz) can chopped plum tomatoes
sprig of sage
250–375 g (8–12 oz) dried bucatini
salt and pepper

Heat the oil in a saucepan, add the onion, garlic and aubergine and cook for 5 minutes, then add the mushrooms and tomatoes, plus the juice from the can. Add the sage and a little salt and pepper. Cover the pan and cook gently for 15 minutes. Remove the sage.

Meanwhile, bring a large pan of salted water to the boil. Add the pasta, stir and cook for about 8 minutes until *al dente*. Drain the pasta and add to the sauce. Heat the pasta with the sauce for 1 minute, stirring gently to blend the two together, then serve at once.

Serves 4

kcal 400; kJ 1703; protein 14 (g); fat 5 (g); CHO 79 (g)

Macaroni in Tomato Sauce

If you don't have any macaroni in your store cupboard, you can substitute any tubular pasta or dried pasta shapes.

1 teaspoon olive oil
2 garlic cloves, crushed
875 g (1¾ lb) tomatoes, skinned and mashed
pinch of sugar
1 tablespoon balsamic vinegar (optional)
375 g (12 oz) dried macaroni
salt and freshly ground black pepper
1 tablespoon chopped parsley

To make the sauce, heat the oil in a heavy pan, add the garlic and fry gently for 5 minutes. Add the tomatoes and sugar with salt and pepper to taste. Bring to the boil, then simmer for 30 minutes. If wished, add the balsamic vinegar at the end and cook for 2 minutes.

Meanwhile, cook the macaroni in plenty of boiling, salted water for about 8 minutes until *al dente*. Drain thoroughly and pile into a warmed serving dish. Pour over the sauce and sprinkle with the parsley.

Serves 4

kcal 345; kJ 1468; protein 12 (g); fat 3 (g); CHO 72 (g)

left: spaghetti with ratatouille sauce

Spaghetti Peperonata

This delicious spaghetti has a fresh, spicy flavour and is perfect for a winter's lunch or supper.

non-fat spray, for spraying
3 onions, finely chopped
2 garlic cloves, finely chopped
425 g (14 oz) can chopped plum tomatoes
1 tablespoon tomato purée
1 tablespoon chopped oregano
2 bay leaves
1 green pepper, cored, deseeded and diced
1 red pepper, cored, deseeded and diced
375 g (12 oz) dried spaghetti
2 tablespoons grated Parmesan cheese
salt and pepper

Spray a saucepan with non-fat spray and place over a low heat. Add the onions and garlic and then cook for 5 minutes. Add the tomatoes with their juice, the tomato purée, oregano, bay leaves and salt and pepper to taste. Simmer for 10 minutes, and then add the peppers. Cook for 10 minutes or until the peppers are just soft. Remove the bay leaves before serving.

Meanwhile, bring a large pan of salted water to the boil. Add the spaghetti, stir and cook for about 8 minutes until *al dente*. Drain the pasta thoroughly, rinse with hot water and drain again. Pile on to a heated dish or 4 individual plates. Top with the peperonata sauce and serve sprinkled with Parmesan.

Serves 4

kcal 411; kJ 1747; protein 16 (g); fat 3 (g); CHO 85 (g)

above: spaghetti peperonata
right: tomato tagliatelle

Tomato Tagliatelle

500 g (1 lb) fresh tomato tagliatelle
1 tablespoon vegetable oil
2 onions, sliced
2 garlic cloves, crushed
500 g (1 lb) courgettes, thinly sliced
1 green pepper, cored, deseeded and
  sliced
2 large tomatoes, skinned and
  chopped
250 g (8 oz) button mushrooms,
  sliced
2 tablespoons chopped parsley
salt and pepper
sprigs of oregano, to garnish

Bring a large saucepan of lightly salted water to the boil. Add the pasta, stir and cook for 3–4 minutes or until *al dente*. Drain the pasta, rinse with hot water to stop it becoming sticky and drain again. Return the pasta to the pan and keep warm.

To make the sauce, heat the oil in a saucepan and cook the onions gently for 3 minutes, stirring once or twice. Add the garlic, courgettes and green pepper and cook for 3 minutes. Add the tomatoes and mushrooms, stir well, cover the pan and simmer for 10 minutes or until the vegetables are tender. Season to taste with salt and pepper and stir in the parsley.

Turn the tagliatelle into a heated serving dish, pour on the sauce and toss well. Garnish with oregano sprigs and serve at once.

Serves 6

kcal 333; kJ 1335; protein 14 (g);
fat 5 (g); CHO 61 (g)

Tagliatelle Sicilienne

1 large aubergine, diced
1 tablespoon olive oil
2 onions, chopped

2 garlic cloves, chopped
425 g (14 oz) can chopped plum
 tomatoes
2 teaspoons chopped basil
3.6 litres (6 pints) water
375 g (12 oz) fresh
 tagliatelle
salt and pepper

Sprinkle the diced aubergine with salt and leave for 30 minutes to remove any bitter taste. Rinse in cold water and then dry well with kitchen paper.

Heat the oil in a saucepan, add the onion, garlic and aubergine and cook for 2–3 minutes. Add the

tomatoes and their juice, together with the basil, and season to taste. Simmer for 15–20 minutes.

Meanwhile, bring the water to the boil in a large pan and add salt to taste. Put in the pasta, stir and cook for 3–4 minutes, or according to the packet instructions, until *al dente*. Drain the pasta, turn it into a warm serving dish and then top with the aubergine sauce.

Serves 4

kcal 370; kJ 1490 ; protein 14 (g); fat 5 (g); CHO 68 (g)

Quick Tomato Sauce

1 teaspoon olive oil

2 onions, finely chopped

2 garlic cloves, crushed

2 x 425 g (14 oz) cans chopped tomatoes

2 teaspoons caster sugar

½ teaspoon Worcestershire sauce (optional)

2 tablespoons chopped fresh or 1 tablespoon dried basil

375 g (12 oz) dried pasta of your choice

salt and pepper

Heat the oil in a saucepan. Add the onions and garlic and cook gently for 5–6 minutes or until tender and golden. Stir in the tomatoes, sugar, Worcestershire sauce, if using, salt

and pepper to taste and the basil. Bring to the boil and cook rapidly for about 5 minutes or until the sauce has thickened.

Meanwhile, cook the pasta in plenty of boiling salted water for about 8–10 minutes, or according to the packet instructions, until *al dente*. Drain well and then mix in the tomato sauce. Serve immediately.

Serves 4

kcal 397; kJ 1687; protein 14 (g); fat 3 (g); CHO 84 (g)

Farfalle with Ricotta and Tomato Sauce

Ricotta is a soft cheese, made from cow's, sheep's or goat's milk, which is frequently used in Italian cookery. It is now sold fresh in most supermarkets as well as Italian delicatessens.

non-fat spray, for spraying

2 garlic cloves, crushed

425 g (14 oz) can chopped tomatoes with herbs

300 g (10 oz) dried farfalle

250 g (8 oz) ricotta or low-fat soft cheese

1 tablespoon freshly grated Parmesan cheese

salt and pepper

basil sprigs, to garnish

Spray a heavy saucepan with non-fat spray and place over a low heat. Add the garlic and fry gently, stirring, for 1–2 minutes until light golden. Add the tomatoes and their juice, stir well and bring to the boil. Reduce the heat and season with salt and pepper to taste. Cover the pan and simmer for 20 minutes.

Bring a large saucepan of salted water to the boil. Add the farfalle, stir well and bring back to the boil. Boil, uncovered, for about 8 minutes or according to the packet instructions, until the pasta is *al dente*.

Meanwhile, put the ricotta in a large bowl, add the grated Parmesan and 3–4 tablespoons of the pasta cooking water. Beat the cheeses together until they are really creamy in consistency.

Drain the farfalle and add to the cheese mixture. Toss well together. Divide the pasta equally between 4 warm soup plates. Taste the tomato sauce and adjust the seasoning. Pour over the pasta and garnish with basil sprigs. Serve at once.

Serves 4

kcal 369; kJ 1564; protein 17 (g); fat 9 (g); CHO 60 (g)

left: tagliatelle Sicilienne

Peperonata with Wholemeal Noodles

Peperonata is a classic dish, combining the best of summer produce – peppers, fresh tomatoes and fresh basil. Use fresh wholemeal noodles if you can – these take about 8–10 minutes to cook, but the extra time is well worth it for the flavour and nutritional benefits.

non-fat spray, for spraying
1 large onion, thinly sliced
1 large garlic clove, crushed
2 red peppers, cored, deseeded and cut into strips
2 green peppers, cored, deseeded and cut into strips
375 g (12 oz) tomatoes, skinned, deseeded and chopped
1 tablespoon chopped fresh basil
175 g (6 oz) fresh wholemeal noodles
salt and pepper
chopped basil, to garnish (optional)

Spray a deep frying pan with non-fat spray and place over a low heat. Add the onion and garlic and cook very gently until the onion is soft but not coloured. Add the peppers, tomatoes, basil and salt and pepper to taste. Cover and cook gently for 10 minutes.

Remove the lid from the pan and then cook over a fairly high heat until most of the moisture has evaporated. Keep the vegetable mixture warm.

Meanwhile, cook the noodles in plenty of boiling salted water for 8–10 minutes, or according to the packet instructions, until *al dente*. Drain thoroughly and add salt and pepper to taste.

Divide the noodles between 4 serving plates and then spoon the hot peperonata over the top. Garnish with sprigs of fresh basil and serve immediately, as a light main course with a salad.

Serves 6

kcal 139; kJ 590; protein 6 (g); fat 1 (g); CHO 28 (g)

left: peperonata with wholemeal noodles
far right: pasta twists with ratatouille sauce

Fusilli with Ratatouille Sauce

Make this vegetable sauce at the end of summer when ratatouille vegetables are at their freshest and best.

1 aubergine, cut into thin strips

non-fat spray, for spraying

1 onion, thinly sliced

1 red pepper, cored, deseeded and halved lengthways

1 yellow pepper, cored, deseeded and halved lengthways

500 g (1 lb) ripe tomatoes, skinned and chopped

2 garlic cloves, crushed

2 tablespoons tomato purée

2 teaspoons chopped basil or parsley

pinch of sugar

300–450 ml (½–¾ pint) vegetable stock

375 g (12 oz) dried wholewheat fusilli

salt and pepper

To garnish:

2 tablespoons grated Parmesan cheese

chopped parsley

Put the aubergine in a colander and sprinkle with salt. Press a plate on top of the strips and weight it down. Leave the aubergine for 20 minutes to remove the bitter taste. Rinse in running cold water and pat dry with kitchen paper.

Meanwhile, spray a heavy pan with non-fat spray and place over a low heat. Add the onion and cook gently, stirring, until it softened – about 5 minutes. Add the peppers, tomatoes and garlic, stirring well.

Add the aubergine with the tomato purée, herbs and sugar. Season with salt and pepper to taste. Bring to the boil, stirring. Reduce the heat, cover the pan and simmer gently for 20 minutes. Add the stock gradually to dilute the sauce as it thickens, and to prevent the vegetables sticking to the pan.

Meanwhile, bring a large saucepan of salted water to the boil, add the fusilli and bring back to the boil.

Reduce the heat slightly and boil. Cook, uncovered, for about 10–12 minutes, or according to the packet instructions, stirring occasionally, until *al dente*. Drain and turn the pasta into a warm serving bowl.

Taste the sauce and adjust the seasoning if necessary. Pour over the pasta. Sprinkle with Parmesan and parsley and serve at once.

Serves 4

kcal 400; kJ 1700; protein 17 (g); fat 5 (g); CHO 78 (g)

Tagliatelle with Chickpea Sauce

If wished, you can soak dried chickpeas overnight before boiling them in plenty of water until cooked and tender. But if you are in a hurry, canned chickpeas are just as good and much more convenient. In a tomato sauce, they go surprisingly well with noodles and pasta ribbons.

425 g (14 oz) can chickpeas, rinsed
   and drained
1 tablespoon olive oil
1 small onion, finely chopped
1 celery stick, diced
2 garlic cloves, finely chopped
1½ x 425 g (14 oz) cans chopped
   tomatoes
2 tablespoons chopped flat leaf
   parsley
1 teaspoon finely chopped rosemary
375 g (12 oz) dried tagliatelle or
   pappardelle
4 tablespoon freshly grated Parmesan
   cheese
salt and pepper

Purée half of the drained chickpeas in a blender, adding a little water if the purée is too thick.

Heat the oil and gently cook the onion and celery until just soft. Add the garlic and then cook until just beginning to colour. Add the tomatoes, parsley, rosemary, salt and pepper. Simmer for 10–15 minutes until thickened. Stir in the puréed and whole chickpeas, and simmer for another 5 minutes.

Meanwhile, cook the pasta in plenty of boiling salted water until *al dente*. Drain and toss with half of the chickpea sauce. Stir in half of the Parmesan cheese.

Transfer the pasta to a serving dish and then spoon the rest of the sauce over the top. Sprinkle with the remaining Parmesan cheese and serve at once.

Serves 6

kcal 335; kJ 1408; protein 14 (g); fat 5 (g); CHO 58 (g)

Spaghetti with Peppers and Olives

1 teaspoon olive oil
1 yellow or green pepper, cored,
   deseeded and sliced
3 tomatoes, skinned and chopped
125 g (4 oz) black olives, pitted and
   halved
425 g (14 oz) dried spaghetti
salt and pepper
25 g (1 oz) grated pecorino or
   Parmesan cheese, to serve

Heat the oil in a heavy pan, add the yellow or green pepper and tomatoes with salt and pepper to taste. Cover and simmer gently for 20 minutes, stirring occasionally. Add the olives and cook for 5 minutes.

Meanwhile, cook the spaghetti in plenty of boiling, salted water for about 8 minutes, or according to the packet instructions, until *al dente*. Drain thoroughly and add to the sauce. Fold gently to mix, then pile into a warmed serving dish and sprinkle with Parmesan. Serve immediately.

Serves 4

kcal 447; kJ 1895; protein 16 (g); fat 8 (g); CHO 82 (g)

Fusilli with Bean Sauce

Mixed bean salad is a combination of green, red kidney, black eye, borlotti and cannellini beans with chickpeas, sweetcorn and red peppers.

1 small onion, finely chopped
185 g (6½ oz) can pimientos (sweet
   red peppers), drained and thinly
   sliced
425 g (14 oz) can chopped tomatoes
   with herbs
425 g (14 oz) can mixed bean salad,
   drained
1 teaspoon tomato purée
375 g (12 oz) dried wholewheat fusilli
2 tablespoons chopped parsley
salt and pepper

right: fusilli with bean sauce

Heat a wok or heavy frying pan and dry-fry the onion for 3–6 minutes, stirring constantly. Add the pimientos and stir-fry for 1–2 minutes. Add the tomatoes with their juice, the beans and tomato purée and season to taste. Stir well and simmer for about 15 minutes.

Meanwhile, bring a large pan of salted water to the boil. Add the pasta, stir and cook for 10–12 minutes, or according to the packet instructions until *al dente*. Drain well and turn into a warm bowl.

Stir half of the parsley into the bean sauce. Adjust the seasoning to taste and then pour the sauce over the pasta, tossing well.

Divide the pasta and its sauce equally among 4 warm bowls, and then scatter over the remaining parsley. Serve at once.

Serves 4

Kcal 362; kJ 1543; protein 16 (g); fat 3 (g); CHO 73

Bean and Fusilli Curry

Curry sauce improves with keeping and can be made the day before. Simply reheat it while the pasta cooks. Serve the curry with some side dishes such as banana slices that have been sprinkled with lemon juice, cucumber slices and mango chutney. The sauce can be reheated and served with rice.

1 tablespoon vegetable oil
3 onions, chopped
2 garlic cloves, crushed
3 tablespoons curry powder
½ teaspoon ground cumin
½ teaspoon ground coriander
½ teaspoon chilli powder
2 teaspoons grated fresh root ginger (optional)
2 tablespoons wholemeal flour
900 ml (1½ pints) vegetable stock
1 tablespoon lemon juice
150 g (5 oz) dried fusilli or penne
2 x 425 g (14 oz) cans red kidney beans
salt and pepper

Heat the oil in a saucepan with a lid and gently fry the onions and garlic for 2–3 minutes. Stir in the curry powder, cumin, coriander, chilli powder, ginger and flour and cook for 1 minute. Pour in the vegetable stock and lemon juice and bring to the boil. Cover and simmer gently for 25 minutes. Add salt to taste.

Meanwhile, bring a large pan of salted water to the boil. Add the pasta, stir and cook for about 10 minutes until *al dente*. Drain and rinse. Drain the canned kidney beans, reserving the liquid for thinning the sauce.

Stir the pasta and beans gently into the sauce. Thin the sauce with the reserved bean liquid, then season to taste and serve.

Serves 4

kcal 436; kJ 1844; protein 21 (g); fat 6 (g); CHO 80 (g)

Spaghetti with Lentil Bolognese Sauce

Unlike some types of lentils, green lentils do not need lengthy pre-soaking. Simply rinse them and then cook.

250 g (8 oz) whole green lentils
2 teaspoons vegetable oil
2 onions, chopped
2 garlic cloves, chopped
2 celery sticks, chopped
2 carrots, finely diced
2 tablespoons tomato purée
375 g (12 oz) dried spaghetti
15 g (½ oz) low-fat spread
salt and pepper

Rinse the lentils in a colander under running cold water, then place in a pan, cover with fresh water and bring to the boil. Reduce the heat and simmer gently for about 40 minutes until tender. Drain the lentils, reserving the liquid.

Heat the oil in a large saucepan, add the onions and cook for 5 minutes until soft, then add the garlic, celery and carrots. Cook the vegetables, covered, for 15 minutes until tender.

Stir in the drained lentils, tomato purée, salt and pepper to taste and a little of the reserved lentil cooking liquid to give the sauce a thick, soft consistency. Simmer the sauce for about 10 minutes, adding more liquid if necessary.

Bring a large saucepan of salted water to the boil. Add the spaghetti, stir and cook vigorously for about 8 minutes, or according to the packet instructions, until *al dente*. Drain the spaghetti, and then return to the saucepan with the low-fat spread and season with freshly ground black pepper.

Make sure that the spaghetti is still really hot, then turn it out on to a hot serving plate and pour the lentil Bolognese sauce over the top.

Serves 4

kcal 439; kJ 1864; protein 18 (g); fat 5 (g); CHO 85 (g)

far left: bean and fusilli curry
above: spaghetti with lentil Bolognese sauce

Spaghetti with Aubergine, Pepper and Olive Sauce

1 tablespoon olive oil
1 onion, finely chopped
425 g (14 oz) can chopped tomatoes
2 tablespoons tomato purée
150 ml (¼ pint) red wine
1 large aubergine, chopped
1 large red pepper, cored, deseeded and finely diced
1 large green pepper, cored, deseeded and finely diced
1 garlic clove, crushed
500 g (1 lb) spaghetti or linguine
75 g (3 oz) pitted black olives
salt and pepper

Heat the oil and fry the onion for 3 minutes. Add the tomatoes, tomato purée, red wine, aubergine, peppers and garlic. Simmer gently for 20 minutes.

Meanwhile, cook the pasta in plenty of boiling salted water for about 8 minutes, until *al dente*. Drain and toss with the sauce, adding the olives and seasoning to taste. Serve at once.

Serves 4–6

kcal 377; kJ 1598; protein 13 (g); fat 6 (g); CHO 69 (g)

Farfalle with Herb and Lemon Sauce

375 g (12 oz) dried farfalle or fusilli
1 tablespoon olive oil
8 spring onions, green parts included, finely chopped
finely grated rind of 1 lemon
75 g (3 oz) trimmed mixed fresh herbs, e.g. flat leaf parsley, rocket, thyme, marjoram, basil, rosemary, chopped
2 tablespoons very low-fat natural fromage frais
4 tablespoons toasted breadcrumbs
25 g (1 oz) freshly grated Parmesan cheese
salt and pepper

Cook the pasta in plenty of boiling salted water for about 8 minutes until *al dente*. Drain well and then transfer to a heated serving dish.

While the pasta is cooking, heat the oil until very hot. Remove from the heat and immediately stir in the spring onions, lemon rind, herbs and fromage frais. Toss with the pasta, breadcrumbs and Parmesan, and season generously with salt and pepper. Serve immediately.

Serves 6

kcal 280; kJ 1190; protein 11 (g); fat 5 (g); CHO 52 (g)

Spaghetti with Three Herb Sauce

3 tablespoons chopped parsley
1 tablespoon chopped tarragon
2 tablespoons chopped basil
1 tablespoon olive oil
1 large garlic clove, crushed
4 tablespoons chicken stock
2 tablespoons dry white wine
375 g (12 oz) multi-coloured dried spaghetti
salt and pepper

Put the parsley, tarragon, basil, olive oil, garlic, chicken stock, white wine and salt and pepper to taste into a food processor or blender and work until smooth.

Cook the spaghetti in a large pan of boiling salted water for about 8 minutes, or according to the packet instructions, until *al dente*. Drain the spaghetti and heap in a warmed bowl. Pour over the herb sauce and toss well, then serve immediately.

Serves 4

kcal 352; kJ 1493; protein 11 (g); fat 5 (g); CHO 67 (g)

right: spaghetti with aubergine, pepper and olive sauce (top); farfalle with herb and lemon sauce

Spaghetti with Mushrooms and Herbs

This is a simple, easy-to-cook lunch or supper dish when you're in a hurry.

2 teaspoons olive oil
75 g (3 oz) onion, finely sliced
1 garlic clove, crushed
175 g (6 oz) mushrooms, finely sliced
1 tablespoon mixed herbs
1 teaspoon dried sage, oregano or
    thyme
2 tablespoons white wine
200 g (7 oz) dried spaghetti
salt and pepper

Heat the oil in a saucepan, add the onion and garlic and fry gently for 2–3 minutes. Add the mushrooms, then the herbs and season with salt and pepper. Continue to fry gently for a few more minutes until the mushrooms have softened and darkened. Add the white wine and simmer for about 5 minutes.

Meanwhile, bring a large pan of salted water to the boil. Add the pasta, stir and cook for about 8 minutes until *al dente*. Drain the pasta and pile into a warmed serving dish. Toss with the sauce and serve immediately.

Serves 2

kcal 405; kJ 1719; protein 14 (g); fat 5 (g); CHO 78 (g)

Italian Vegetable Pasta

1 tablespoon oil
1 onion, finely chopped
1 red pepper, cored, deseeded and
    finely chopped
1 yellow pepper, cored, deseeded and
    finely chopped
2 celery sticks, finely chopped
1 courgette, finely chopped
4 tomatoes, skinned, deseeded and
    chopped
250 g (8 oz) spinach leaves, chopped
150 ml (¼ pint) vegetable stock
1 teaspoon caster sugar
375 g (12 oz) tagliatelle or fettuccine
salt and pepper

Heat the oil in a large saucepan. Add the onion, peppers, celery and courgette and cook for 2 minutes.

Stir in the tomatoes, spinach and stock. Season with some salt and pepper and the sugar. Bring to the boil and then cook rapidly for 10 minutes until the sauce has reduced and is thick.

Meanwhile, cook the pasta in a large pan of boiling salted water for about 8 minutes, or according to the packet instructions, until *al dente*. Drain well and toss with the vegetable sauce. Pile into a serving dish and serve at once.

Serves 4

kcal 386; kJ 1638; protein 14 (g); fat 5 (g); CHO 75 (g)

Fusilli with Fresh Mixed Herbs

400 g (13 oz) dried fusilli
250 g (8 oz) low-fat soft cheese
2 tablespoons chopped thyme
2 tablespoons chopped parsley
1 tablespoon chopped oregano
1 tablespoon chopped mint
1 tablespoon shredded basil
1 small garlic clove, finely chopped
salt and freshly ground black pepper
1 teaspoon freshly grated pecorino
    cheese, to serve

Cook the fusilli in a large saucepan of boiling salted water for about 10 minutes, or according to the packet instructions, until *al dente*. Drain the pasta in a colander but reserve a little of the cooking water to thin down the sauce.

Beat the soft cheese with the herbs, garlic and season with salt and pepper. Tip the pasta into a warm serving dish and then toss with the cheese and herb mixture. Serve immediately with grated pecorino cheese.

Serves 4

kcal 440; kJ 1866; protein 19 (g); fat 9 (g); CHO 76 (g)

far left: spaghetti with mushrooms and herbs

Conchiglie with Spicy Broccoli Sauce

500 g (1 lb) broccoli florets
500 g (1 lb) dried conchiglie or fusilli

dried chilli flakes, to serve
3 tablespoons very low-fat natural fromage frais
50 g (2 oz) freshly grated Parmesan cheese
salt and freshly ground black pepper

Cook the broccoli florets in boiling lightly salted water for 3 minutes until just tender. Drain and break into smaller pieces. Dice the stalks.

Meanwhile, cook the pasta in plenty of boiling salted water, for about 10 minutes, or according to the packet instructions, until *al dente*. Drain and transfer to a warm serving dish, reserving a little of the pasta water to thin the sauce.

Add the broccoli, salt and pepper, chilli flakes, fromage frais and half of the Parmesan to the pan. Mix well, adding a little of the pasta water if necessary to keep the mixture moist.

Toss the sauce gently with the cooked pasta and serve immediately with the remaining Parmesan.

Serves 6

kcal 358; kJ 1516; protein 18 (g); fat 5 (g); CHO 64 (g)

Conchiglie with Cauliflower Sauce

1 cauliflower, broken into florets
1 tablespoon olive oil
2 garlic cloves, cut into 3–4 pieces
10 black olives, pitted and quartered
1 tablespoon capers
500 g (1 lb) dried conchiglie
salt

left: conchiglie with spicy broccoli sauce

Prepare the sauce before cooking the pasta. Boil the cauliflower in salted water until almost cooked, then strain, reserving about 150 ml (¼ pint) of the cooking water.

Heat the olive oil and fry the garlic gently until golden. Add the olives and capers and fry gently for about 5 minutes, until they have begun to soften. Add the strained cauliflower and stir well, adding the reserved cooking water to keep the mixture moist.

Cook the conchiglie in boiling salted water for about 8 minutes and drain it 2–3 minutes before it becomes *al dente*. Add to the cauliflower sauce in the pan and finish cooking the pasta in the cauliflower sauce, adding a little pasta cooking water if necessary to keep the mixture moist.

Serves 4

kcal 492; kJ 2088; protein 18 (g); fat 7 (g); CHO 95 (g)

Pasta with Grilled Vegetable Sauce

non-fat spray, for spraying
8 ripe tomatoes, halved and deseeded
1 red pepper, cored, deseeded and cut in strips
1 yellow pepper, cored, deseeded and cut in strips

2 onions, thickly sliced
4 garlic cloves, unpeeled
1 teaspoon chopped thyme
½ teaspoon chopped rosemary
375 g (12 oz) dried ribbon pasta, e.g. tagliatelle or fettuccine
salt and freshly ground black pepper
2 tablespoons chopped parsley, to serve

Spray a cast-iron ridged grill pan or the inside of a conventional grill pan which sits under an overhead grill with non-fat spray.

Put all the prepared vegetables, garlic and herbs in the pan and season with salt and pepper. Place the cast-iron pan over a medium heat or place under a preheated hot grill and cook until the vegetables start to look slightly charred and are tender and sweet. Turn them occasionally during cooking.

Squeeze the garlic cloves out of their skins and discard the skins. Tip all the grilled vegetables into a frying pan and simmer for 3–4 minutes, until the tomatoes go pulpy.

Meanwhile, cook the pasta in plenty of boiling salted water for about 8 minutes, or according to the packet instructions, until *al dente*. Drain well and toss with the grilled vegetable sauce. Serve scattered with chopped parsley.

Serves 4

kcal 400; kJ 1675; protein 14 (g); fat 2 (g); CHO 83 (g)

Tagliatelle Napoletana

500 g (1 lb) ripe tomatoes
1 teaspoon olive oil
1 large onion, chopped
2 garlic cloves, crushed
1 tablespoon chopped fresh oregano
14 black olives
1 tablespoon capers
375 g (12 oz) tagliatelle or fettuccine
salt and black pepper
2 tablespoons chopped basil

Put the tomatoes in a roasting pan and bake in a preheated oven, 180°C (350°F), Gas Mark 4, for 12–15 minutes until softened and the skins are slightly charred. Remove the skins and chop the flesh roughly.

Heat the olive oil in a large saucepan, add the onion and garlic and sauté gently for about 5 minutes until soft and golden. Add the tomatoes, oregano, olives and capers, and simmer gently for about 10 minutes until slightly thickened.

Meanwhile, cook the pasta in boiling lightly salted water for about 8 minutes until *al dente*. Drain thoroughly and divide between 4 serving plates. Top with the tomato sauce and serve sprinkled with basil.

Serves 4

kcal 390; kJ 1627; protein 14 (g); fat 4 (g); CHO 77 (g)

Linguine with Aubergine, Tomato and Chilli Sauce

non-fat spray, for spraying
1 large aubergine, cut into 1 cm
  (½ inch) cubes
2 garlic cloves, finely chopped
1 fresh chilli, deseeded and chopped
2 x 425 g (14 oz) cans chopped
  tomatoes
3 tablespoons chopped flat leaf parsley
500 g (1 lb) linguine or fettuccine
salt and pepper
freshly grated Parmesan cheese, to
  garnish

Spray a large pan with non-fat spray and place over a low heat. Add the aubergine and gently fry for about 5 minutes. Stir in the garlic and chilli and cook until the garlic begins to colour. Stir in the tomatoes and parsley. Season with salt and pepper and simmer for about 30 minutes.

Meanwhile, cook the pasta in boiling salted water for about 8 minutes until *al dente*. Drain and toss with half of the sauce. Transfer to a serving dish, and spoon over the remaining sauce. Dust with Parmesan and serve at once.

Serves 4

kcal 490; kJ 2088; protein 19 (g);
fat 4 (g); CHO 100 (g)

Farfalle with Herbed Savoy Cabbage

1 tablespoon olive oil
2 garlic cloves, finely chopped
875 g (1¾ lb) Savoy cabbage,
  shredded
finely grated rind of 1 lemon
3 tablespoons chopped flat leaf
  parsley
1 tablespoon chopped dill
1 tablespoon chopped mint
2–3 tablespoons very low fat natural
  fromage frais
500 g (1 lb) dried farfalle or fusilli
4 tablespoons freshly grated
  Parmesan cheese
salt and pepper

Heat the oil and gently fry the garlic and cabbage for 2 minutes. Season the cabbage to taste with salt and pepper, then cover the pan and cook over a medium heat for 10 minutes, until the cabbage is tender but still crisp. Uncover the pan and raise the heat. Stir in the lemon rind, herbs and fromage frais.

Meanwhile, cook the pasta in plenty of boiling salted water for about 10 minutes, until *al dente*. Drain and toss with the cabbage. Stir in the Parmesan.

Serves 6

kcal 376; kJ 1595 ; protein 16 (g);
fat 6 (g); CHO 68 (g)

Pasta with Vegetable Sauce

2 courgettes, diced
1 aubergine, diced
1 large onion, chopped
1 red or green pepper, cored,
  deseeded and chopped
2 teaspoons oil
375 g (12 oz) plum tomatoes, skinned
  and chopped
250 ml (8 fl oz) vegetable stock
1 tablespoon chopped parsley
375 g (12 oz) dried pasta of your
  choice
salt and pepper

Cook the courgettes, aubergine, onion and pepper in the oil in a large pan, stirring occasionally, for 10 minutes over a low heat.

Add the tomatoes, vegetable stock and seasoning. Simmer for 30 minutes and stir in the parsley just before removing from the heat.

Cook the pasta in plenty of boiling salted water for about 8–10 minutes, or according to the packet instructions, until *al dente*. Drain well and then toss with the vegetable sauce

Serves 4

kcal 367; kJ 1560; protein 12 (g);
fat 4 (g); CHO 75 (g)

right: linguine with aubergine, tomato and chilli sauce (top); farfalle with herbed Savoy cabbage

Conchiglie with Broad Beans and Greens

This lovely fresh green dish makes a light, refreshing meal in late spring or early summer when broad beans and spring greens are at their seasonal best. Of course, you could could use frozen or canned broad beans but they won't be nearly so good as fresh ones.

250 g (8 oz) shelled young broad beans

875 g (1¾ lb) spring greens, kale or Swiss chard

non-fat spray, for spraying

1 red onion, finely chopped

3 garlic cloves, finely chopped

3 sage leaves, finely chopped

½ teaspoon dried chilli flakes

500 g (1 lb) dried conchiglie, penne or gnocchi

4 tablespoons freshly grated Parmesan cheese

salt and pepper

Plunge the broad beans into boiling water for 2 minutes. Drain under cold running water, then slip off the outer skins if they are tough. Remove the tough stalks from the spring greens, kale or chard and finely slice the leaves crossways.

Spray a large pan with non-fat spray, heat gently and then add the onion. Cook over a low heat, stirring occasionally, until just soft.

Add the garlic, sage and chilli flakes. Add the greens and toss the leaves gently. Cover and cook over a medium heat for 7–10 minutes, until the greens are just tender, adding a little water if the mixture becomes too dry. Stir in the broad beans and season to taste.

Cook the pasta in plenty of boiling salted water for about 10 minutes until *al dente*. Drain and toss with the vegetables. Stir in the Parmesan, transfer to a serving dish and serve at once.

Serves 6

kcal 395; kJ 1673; protein 19 (g); fat 5 (g); CHO 73 (g)

---

left: *conchiglie with broad beans and greens*
below: *tagliatelle with leek and green peppercorn sauce*

Tagliatelle with Leek and Green Peppercorn Sauce

non-fat spray, for spraying
750 g (1½ lb) leeks, sliced lengthways and cut into matchstick strips
2 tablespoons green peppercorns, crushed
3 tablespoons chopped parsley
300 ml (½ pint) very low-fat natural fromage frais
500 g (1 lb) dried tagliatelle
4 tablespoons freshly grated Parmesan cheese
salt

Spray a pan with non-fat spray and place over a low heat. Add the leeks and green peppercorns and cook gently for 3–4 minutes until the leeks are just tender. Stir in the parsley and fromage frais, and season to taste with salt. Cook very gently over a low heat to heat through.

Cook the pasta in plenty of boiling salted water for about 8 minutes until *al dente*. Drain and toss with the sauce. Stir in the Parmesan and serve at once.

Serves 4

kcal 540; kJ 2300; protein 26 (g); fat 5 (g); CHO 103 (g)

Penne with Spring Vegetables

You can add virtually any fresh spring vegetables to this pasta dish. Try thin green beans, mangetout, asparagus tips and fresh peas or broad beans.

200 g (7 oz) broccoli florets, divided into tiny sprigs

4 young carrots, thinly sliced

200 g (7 oz) frozen petits pois

375 g (12 oz) dried penne

200 g (7 oz) small button mushrooms, quartered

6 tablespoons dry white wine

2 tablespoons finely chopped parsley

300 ml (½ pint) very low-fat natural yogurt

salt and pepper

1 tablespoon freshly grated Parmesan cheese, to serve

Cook the broccoli and carrots in a pan of boiling salted water for 5–7 minutes until they are tender but still crunchy. Remove with a slotted spoon and drain. Add the petits pois to the water and bring back to the boil. Simmer for 3–4 minutes, then remove and drain well.

Bring a large saucepan of salted water to the boil. Add the penne, stir and cook vigorously for about 10 minutes until *al dente*.

While the pasta is cooking, put the mushrooms, wine and parsley in a saucepan and season with salt and pepper. Cook for about 10 minutes until *al dente*, stirring. Add the vegetables and toss over a high heat to heat through.

Drain the penne thoroughly and turn into a warm bowl. Add the yogurt and vegetables and toss quickly together. Divide the pasta equally among 4 warm soup bowls. Sprinkle the Parmesan on top and serve at once.

Serves 4

kcal 577; kJ 2450; protein 28 (g); fat 6 (g); CHO 109 (g)

Penne Primavera

Other vegetables that would be delicious in Penne Primavera include fennel, mushrooms, fresh peas, cauliflower, asparagus or red pepper.

125 g (4 oz) broccoli, broken into small pieces
125 g (4 oz) French beans, cut into 5 cm (2 inch) lengths
125 g (4 oz) mangetout
2 tablespoons chopped herbs
500 g (1 lb) dried penne
Vinaigrette:
3 teaspoons olive oil
2 tablespoons cider or wine vinegar
2 teaspoons French mustard or 1 teaspoon English mustard
1 teaspoon caster sugar
freshly grated nutmeg (optional)
1 garlic clove, crushed (optional)
salt and pepper

Steam all the vegetables for 2–4 minutes until slightly softened but still brightly coloured and crisp. Drain and put into a large bowl.

To make the vinaigrette, blend together all the ingredients and pour over the vegetables. Sprinkle the vegetables with herbs.

Meanwhile, bring a large pan of salted water to the boil. Add the pasta, stir and cook for about 10 minutes, or according to the packet instructions, until *al dente*. Drain, and mix into the bowl of vegetables and vinaigrette. Serve hot or cold.

Serves 4

kcal 489; kJ 2079; protein 18 (g); fat 5 (g); CHO 99 (g)

far left: penne with spring vegetables
above: penne primavera

Rigatoni with Courgette Sauce

If courgette flowers are available, they can be washed, sliced and added to the courgettes and onions while frying. The edible flowers have a delicate flavour and a deep orange colour.

2 teaspoons olive oil
2 onions, finely chopped
8 courgettes, thinly sliced
500 g (1 lb) dried rigatoni
1 tablespoon freshly grated Parmesan
  cheese
salt and pepper
roughly chopped oregano, to garnish

Heat the oil in a large frying pan, add the onions and fry gently for about 5 minutes until soft and transparent. Add the courgettes after 3 minutes and fry them gently until just tender, stirring frequently to prevent them sticking. Cover the pan if the courgettes start to burn on the outside before being cooked through. Season to taste.

Meanwhile, bring a large pan of salted water to the boil. Add the rigatoni, stir and cook for about 10 minutes, or according to the packet instructions, until *al dente*. Drain the pasta, reserving a small quantity of the cooking water.

Transfer the rigatoni to a warmed serving dish and then mix in the courgettes and onions, adding a ladleful of the cooking water and the Parmesan to form a moist, creamy mixture. Serve immediately, garnished with oregano.

Serves 4

kcal 490; kJ 2085; protein 18 (g);
fat 5 (g); CHO 101 (g)

above: rigatoni with courgette sauce
right: spaghetti with rocket and ricotta

Spaghetti with Rocket and Ricotta

Rocket has become very fashionable in recent years. Its hot, peppery flavour adds an interesting and delicious touch to a ricotta sauce that is more usually made with fresh spinach leaves.

300 g (10 oz) dried spaghetti
2 teaspoons olive oil
1 small onion, finely chopped
1 bunch of rocket, roots trimmed and leaves finely chopped
1 garlic clove, finely chopped
75 g (3 oz) ricotta cheese
125 ml (4 fl oz) dry white wine
salt and pepper

Plunge the spaghetti into a large saucepan of salted boiling water and cook for about 8 minutes, or according to the packet instructions, until *al dente*.

Meanwhile, heat the oil, then add the onion and cook gently, stirring, for 5 minutes until softened. Add the rocket, garlic and some salt and pepper to taste and stir for 2–3 minutes until the rocket is wilted.

Add the ricotta and wine and stir until the ricotta has melted and is mixed evenly with the rocket.

Drain the spaghetti, return to the pan and add the rocket mixture. Toss well to combine and serve.

Serves 4

kcal 330; kJ 1394; protein 12 (g); fat 5 (g); CHO 58 (g)

Spinach Spaghetti

This makes a really quick and easy vegetarian-style supper dish. Although fresh chopped spinach leaves are best, you could use frozen spinach instead if you're in a hurry.

250 g (8 oz) low-fat dried spaghetti
1 onion, chopped
250 g (8 oz) spinach, chopped
150 ml (¼ pint) very low-fat natural yogurt
125 g (4 oz) vegetarian Quark cheese
1 teaspoon lemon juice
¼ teaspoon grated nutmeg
salt and pepper

Bring a large saucepan of salted water to the boil. Add the pasta, stir and cook for about 10 minutes, or according to the packet instructions, until *al dente*.

Meanwhile, dry-fry the onion, turning constantly, until soft but not browned. Add the spinach and cook for 2–3 minutes. Stir in the yogurt, Quark, lemon juice, nutmeg and salt and pepper and cook over a low heat without boiling.

Drain the pasta and stir into the hot spinach sauce. Toss them gently together and then serve at once.

Serves 3

kcal 386; kJ 1616; protein 22 (g); fat 2 (g); CHO 71 (g)

Spaghetti with Garlic and Chilli Sauce

non-fat spray, for spraying
4 garlic cloves, finely chopped
1 fresh red chilli, deseeded and finely
  chopped
500 g (1 lb) dried spaghetti
2 tablespoons chopped parsley
freshly ground black pepper

Spray a saucepan with non-fat spray and place over a low heat. Fry the garlic and chilli for 1–2 minutes until the garlic is pale golden. Do not allow it to brown.

Meanwhile, cook the spaghetti in plenty of boiling salted water for about 8 minutes, or according to the packet instructions, until *al dente*. Drain and toss with the garlic and chilli mixture and the parsley. Season with black pepper and serve immediately.

Serves 6

kcal 288; kJ 1226; protein 10 (g); fat 2 (g); CHO 62 (g)

left: *spinach spaghetti*
right: *spaghetti with garlic and chilli sauce*

Penne with Asparagus Sauce

Simple and delicious, this is one of the best and most healthy pasta dishes.

1 kg (2 lb) asparagus
15 g (½ oz) butter
500 g (1 lb) dried penne
25 g (1 oz) freshly grated Parmesan
   cheese
4–5 tablespoons very low-fat natural
   fromage frais
salt and pepper

Start making the sauce before you cook the penne. Boil the asparagus in plenty of salted water until cooked, but not too soft. Discard the stalks, leaving only the green and purple spears. Cut these into 2.5 cm (1 inch) lengths. Melt the butter and sauté the asparagus for a few minutes until just tender.

Cook the penne in plenty of boiling salted water for about 10 minues until *al dente*. Drain, transfer to a serving dish and add the asparagus with the grated Parmesan. Mix well, adding the fromage frais to keep the mixture moist. Season with salt and pepper and serve immediately.

Serves 4

kcal 569; kJ 2410; protein 27 (g);
fat 9 (g); CHO 102 (g)

Tagliatelle with Radicchio

1 tablespoon olive oil
1 onion, finely chopped
250 g (8 oz) radicchio, finely shredded
150 ml (¼ pint) very low-fat natural
   fromage frais
300 g (10 oz) fresh tagliatelle
25 g (1 oz) freshly grated Parmesan
   cheese
salt and pepper

Heat the oil in a large heavy pan. Add the onion and cook gently, until softened. Add the radicchio, reserving a few small curly inner leaves for the garnish, and cook, stirring, over a moderate heat, until it wilts and begins to turn brown. Season to taste. Stir in the fromage frais and heat through gently.

Plunge the pasta into a pan of boiling salted water, stir and bring back to the boil. Boil, uncovered, for about 3–4 minutes, stirring occasionally, until *al dente*. Drain the tagliatelle well and place in a warm serving bowl.

Taste the sauce and adjust the seasoning if necessary. Pour the sauce over the pasta and add the Parmesan. Toss quickly to combine. Serve, garnished with the reserved radicchio leaves.

Serves 4

kcal 330; kJ 1329; protein 16 (g);
fat 7 (g); CHO 52 (g)

Penne with Spicy Olive Sauce

500 g (1 lb) dried penne
1 tablespoon olive oil
½ teaspoon ground ginger
generous pinch of grated nutmeg
1 garlic clove, crushed
3 tablespoons capers
75 g (3 oz) pitted black olives, sliced
2 tablespoons chopped parsley
salt and pepper
basil sprigs, to garnish

Cook the penne in plenty of boiling salted water for about 10 minutes, or according to the packet instructions, until *al dente*. Drain thoroughly.

Return the cooked penne to the pan, together with the oil, ginger, nutmeg, a good grinding of pepper, garlic, capers, olives and parsley. Add salt to taste.

Stir the pasta over a gentle heat for 1–2 minutes. Serve immediately, garnished with basil sprigs.

Serves 4

kcal 480; kJ 2043; protein 15 (g);
fat 7 (g); CHO 95 (g)

far left: penne with asparagus sauce

Spaghetti with Courgette and Carrot Ribbons

In this unusual recipe, carrots and courgettes are cut into long, thin strips which echo the shape of the spaghetti.

3 carrots
3 courgettes
1 tablespoon olive oil
2 garlic cloves, crushed
300 g (10 oz) dried spaghetti
75 g (3 oz) finely chopped basil
40 g (1½ oz) finely chopped parsley
25 g (1 oz) snipped chives
2 tablespoons chopped marjoram
½ small radicchio, shredded
salt and pepper
25 g (1 oz) Parmesan shavings, to
    garnish

Using a vegetable peeler, slice the carrots and courgettes into long thin strips, to resemble spaghetti.

Heat the oil in a large frying pan. Add the garlic and carrots and sauté, stirring, for 5 minutes.

Meanwhile, bring a large pan of lightly salted water to the boil. Add the spaghetti and cook for about 8 minutes, or according to the packet instructions, until *al dente*. Drain and add to the pan with the courgette, basil, parsley, chives, marjoram, salt and pepper. Stir to mix and cook for 4–5 minutes until the courgettes are cooked through. Remove from the heat and pile the spaghetti and vegetable mixture onto a warmed serving dish. Add the shredded radicchio and toss to mix. Sprinkle with the Parmesan shavings and serve immediately.

Serves 4

kcal 343; kJ 1452; protein 13 (g);
fat 7 (g); CHO 61 (g)

Sorrel Sauce

125 g (4 oz) sorrel
300 ml (½ pint) vegetable stock
175 ml (6 fl oz) very low-fat natural
    yogurt
375 g (12 oz) dried ribbon pasta
salt and pepper

Cut out and discard the central stalks of the sorrel and chop the leaves. Simmer for 5 minutes in the stock, then allow to cool slightly and purée until smooth in a blender. Mix the sorrel purée with the yogurt and heat through gently without boiling. Season to taste with salt and pepper.

Meanwhile, cook the pasta in plenty of boiling salted water for about 8 minutes, or according to the packet instructions, until *al dente*. Drain well and toss with the sorrel sauce. Serve at once.

Serves 4

kcal 357; kJ 1493; protein 14 (g);
fat 2 (g); CHO 72 (g)

Penne with Olives

425 g (14 oz) dried penne
1 tablespoon olive oil
1 small onion, finely chopped
1 celery stick, finely chopped
1 red pepper, cored, deseeded and
    finely chopped
2 tablespoons dry white wine
2 tablespoons black olive purée
50 g (2 oz) pitted black olives,
    chopped
6 tablespoons very low-fat natural
    fromage frais
2 tablespoons Gruyère cheese
salt and pepper

Cook the penne in plenty of salted boiling water for about 10 minutes until *al dente*.

Meanwhile, cook the vegetables in the oil until golden. Add the wine, simmer gently until it evaporates, then mix in the olive purée, olives and fromage frais.

Drain the pasta and return it to the pan with the sauce. Add the Gruyère and mix gently together. Season to taste, leave on a low heat to heat through and then pour into a large serving dish.

Serves 4

kcal 480; kJ 2039; protein 18 (g);
fat 9 (g); CHO 86 (g)

right: spaghetti with courgette and carrot ribbons

Spaghetti with Saffron

Saffron is more commonly used in risottos than with pasta. Here it adds a beautiful golden colour.

425 g (14 oz) spaghetti or linguine
1 large pinch of saffron threads
1 teaspoon oil
½ large onion, finely chopped
150 ml (¼ pint) very low-fat natural fromage frais
salt and pepper

Bring a large saucepan of salted water to the boil. Add the spaghetti or linguine, stir and bring back to the boil. Boil, uncovered, for about 8 minutes, or according to the packet instructions, stirring occasionally, until *al dente*.

Meanwhile, put the saffron threads in a heatproof bowl. Stir in 2 tablespoons of the pasta cooking water and leave the saffron to soak. Heat the oil and cook the onion very gently, stirring frequently, until golden. Remove the pan from the heat. Strain in the saffron liquid and stir in the fromage frais, mixing well to blend the ingredients.

Drain the pasta well and turn it into a warm bowl. Stir the saffron sauce into the hot pasta and season with salt and pepper to taste, tossing it well. Serve at once.

Serves 4

kcal 403; kJ 1702; protein 16 (g); fat 3 (g); CHO 84 (g)

Persian Noodles with Aubergine

1 large aubergine, thickly sliced
600 ml (1 pint) vegetable stock
125 g (4 oz) dried noodles
4 courgettes, sliced
1 teaspoon ground mace
salt and pepper

Place the aubergine slices in a colander set over a plate, sprinkle with salt and leave for 30 minutes to exude their bitter juice. Rinse the aubergine, drain and pat dry with kitchen paper, then chop into bite-sized pieces.

Put the stock in a large saucepan and bring to the boil. Add the noodles and cook for 5 minutes, then add the aubergine, courgettes, mace and pepper to taste.

Reduce the heat and then simmer gently for a further 10–15 minutes until the noodles and vegetables are tender. Season with salt and pepper to taste, if required. Drain and serve immediately.

Serves 4

kcal 132; kJ 560; protein 5 (g); fat 1 (g); CHO 27 (g)

Chinese-style Vermicelli

Vermicelli is a particularly thread-like pasta, more often used in soups. Here it is tossed with vegetables and an oriental-style sauce flavoured with ginger, garlic, honey and soy sauce.

250 g (8 oz) dried vermicelli
4 carrots, cut into fine matchsticks
4 courgettes, cut into fine matchsticks
125 g (4 oz) small mangetout
2 teaspoons oil
4 spring onions, sliced diagonally
2.5 cm (1 inch) piece of fresh root
  ginger, peeled and sliced into
  matchsticks
1–2 garlic cloves, crushed
4 tablespoons light soy sauce
1 tablespoon clear honey
1 tablespoon white wine vinegar
1 teaspoon coriander seeds, crushed
salt and pepper
parsley leaves, to garnish

Bring a large saucepan of salted water to the boil, then add the vermicelli, stir and bring back to the boil. Reduce the heat slightly and boil, uncovered, for about 8 minutes, or according to the packet instructions, until *al dente*, stirring occasionally.

Meanwhile, put the carrots, courgettes and mangetout into a colander or sieve and sprinkle with salt. Place the colander over the pan of boiling vermicelli. Cover the colander and steam the vegetables for about 5 minutes until they are tender but still crunchy. Remove the colander and set it aside. Drain the vermicelli and cut it into shorter lengths with kitchen scissors.

Heat the oil in a wok or a deep frying pan. Add the spring onions and ginger and cook gently, stirring, until the ingredients release a spicy aroma. Add the garlic, soy sauce, honey, wine vinegar and coriander seeds, stirring well.

Add the vermicelli and vegetables. Increase the heat and vigorously toss the ingredients in the wok until they are evenly combined and hot. Season with pepper to taste. Turn into a warm serving bowl, garnish with parsley leaves and serve.

Serves 4

kcal 297; kJ 1243; protein 9 (g); fat 2 (g); CHO 61 (g)

far left: spaghetti with saffron

Fish and Seafood Sauces

Trenette with Anchovies

Anchovies are very salty and a few go a long way! Most anchovies are bought canned in oil. If so, drain well and pat dry before using. Alternatively, you can buy anchovies in brine. These need to be thoroughly rinsed and dried to remove the salty taste.

1 tablespoon olive oil
2 garlic cloves, crushed
2 large onions, finely chopped
1 red pepper, skinned, cored, deseeded and cut into strips
1 yellow pepper, skinned, cored, deseeded and cut into strips
425g (14 oz) can plum tomatoes, drained, seeded and chopped
40 g (1½ oz) can anchovies, drained and chopped
pinch of sugar
500 g (1 lb) dried trenette
2 tablespoons Parmesan cheese, grated
1 tablespoon chopped parsley
salt and pepper

Heat the oil in a pan and cook the garlic and onions until soft and just beginning to colour. Add the red and yellow peppers and cook until soft, then add the tomatoes and anchovies. Season with pepper and add the sugar. Cook for a few minutes until the tomatoes and anchovies are heated through.

Meanwhile, cook the trenette in plenty of boiling salted water for about 8 minutes, or according to the packet instructions, until *al dente*. Drain well. Place in a hot serving dish and stir in a little sauce and half of the Parmesan.

Just before serving, pour the rest of the sauce over the trenette and then sprinkle with the remaining Parmesan and chopped parsley. Serve at once.

Serves 4

kcal 577; kJ 2447; protein 22 (g); fat 9 (g); CHO 110 (g)

Spaghetti alla Puttanesca

1 tablespoon olive oil
2 cloves garlic, crushed
1 small dried red chilli, deseeded and chopped
6 anchovy fillets, chopped
500 g (1 lb) ripe tomatoes, skinned, deseeded and chopped
50 g (2 oz) black olives, pitted and halved
2 tablespoons capers
375 g (12 oz) dried spaghetti
salt

In a saucepan, heat the oil and add the garlic, chilli and anchovies. Cook gently for 1 minute. Stir in the tomatoes, olives and capers, bring to the boil and simmer for about 10 minutes until thickened. Cook the spaghetti in a large pan of boiling salted water for about 8 minutes, or according to the packet instructions, until *al dente*. Drain well, toss with the sauce and serve immediately.

Serves 4

kcal 389; kJ 1652; protein 13 (g); fat 7 (g); CHO 73 (g)

Tuna and Mushroom Sauce

1 tablespoon olive oil
1 garlic clove, crushed
250 g (8 oz) mushrooms, finely sliced
1 small red pepper, cored, deseeded and thinly sliced
200 g (7 oz) can tuna in brine, drained and flaked
500 g (1 lb) dried penne or macaroni
salt and pepper
finely chopped parsley or basil, to garnish

Heat the oil in a pan and gently fry the garlic, mushrooms and pepper for 5 minutes, until the vegetables are tender but still firm. Add the tuna to the pan and stir gently until the sauce is blended and heated through. Season to taste with salt and pepper.

Cook the pasta in boiling salted water for about 10 minutes, or according to packet instructions, until *al dente*. Drain and toss with half of the sauce. Transfer to a serving dish and spoon the remaining sauce over. Garnish with chopped parsley or basil and serve.

Serves 6

kcal 350; kJ 1490; protein 19 (g); fat 4 (g); CHO 64 (g)

above: *trenette with anchovies*

Spaghetti with Anchovies

500 g (1 lb) dried spaghetti

2 x 50 g (2 oz) cans anchovies in brine, drained, rinsed and chopped

1 garlic clove, crushed

finely grated rind and juice of 1 orange

pinch of sugar

½ tablespoon freshly grated Parmesan cheese

2 tablespoons chopped mint

salt and pepper

Bring a large saucepan of salted water to the boil. Add the spaghetti, stir and cook for about 8 minutes, or according to the packet instructions, until *al dente*.

Put the anchovies in a pan with the garlic. Place over a low heat and stir with a wooden spoon, pressing the anchovies so that they break up and become almost puréed. Add the orange rind and juice, the sugar and pepper to taste. Stir vigorously until the sauce is heated through and combined with the anchovies.

Drain the spaghetti well and turn it into a warmed serving bowl. Pour over the sauce, add the Parmesan and half of the mint and then toss together quickly. Serve at once, sprinkled with the remaining mint.

Serves 6

kcal 344; kJ 1460; protein 15 (g); fat 5 (g); CHO 64 (g)

above: spaghetti with anchovies
right: pasta Syracuse style

Pasta Syracuse Style

1 large onion, sliced

2 garlic cloves, crushed

500 g (1 lb) courgettes, chopped

1 green pepper, cored, deseeded and chopped

425 g (14 oz) can tomatoes, drained and roughly chopped

125 g (4 oz) black olives, pitted

3 anchovy fillets, finely chopped

1 tablespoon chopped parsley

2 teaspoons chopped marjoram

375 g (12 oz) low-fat dried pasta

salt and pepper

few sprigs of flat leaf parsley, to garnish

Heat a large frying pan and dry-fry the onion and garlic for 3–6 minutes, turning constantly, until soft. Add the courgettes and cook for 10 minutes. Add the green pepper, tomatoes, olives, anchovies, parsley, marjoram and salt and pepper to taste. Bring to the boil, stirring, then cover the pan, reduce the heat and simmer while cooking the pasta.

Bring a large saucepan of salted water to the boil. Add the pasta, stir and cook for 8 minutes, or according to the packet instructions, until *al dente*. Drain well and place in a warm serving dish. Add the sauce and toss lightly together. Garnish with the parsley and serve at once.

Serves 4

kcal 427; kJ 1810; protein 16 (g); fat 6 (g); CHO 84 (g)

Spaghetti with Sardines

1 onion, chopped

500 g (1 lb) tomatoes, skinned and chopped

1 garlic clove, crushed

½ teaspoon saffron, soaked in 4 tablespoons boiling water

150 g (5 oz) can sardines in brine

500 g (1 lb) dried spaghetti

salt and pepper

Heat a frying pan or wok and dry-fry the onion, turning constantly for 3–6 minutes, until soft. Add the tomatoes, garlic, the saffron with its water, sardines and salt and pepper to taste, then simmer gently over a low heat for 20 minutes.

Bring a large saucepan of salted water to the boil. Add the pasta, stir and cook for about 8 minutes, or according to the packet instructions, until *al dente*. Drain and mix with the sardine sauce. Serve immediately.

Serves 6

kcal 350; kJ 1492; protein 16 (g); fat 4 (g); CHO 66 (g)

left: spaghetti with sardines

Pasta with Piquant Sauce

2 teaspoons olive oil

1 large onion, chopped

8 anchovy fillets, finely chopped

2 tablespoons chopped parsley

1 garlic clove, finely chopped

1 celery stick, finely chopped

½ teaspoon dried rosemary

½ teaspoon dried sage

500 g (1 lb) tomatoes, skinned and diced

150 ml (¼ pint) dry white wine

¾ teaspoon salt

½ teaspoon pepper

375 g (12 oz) dried ribbon pasta

2 tablespoons grated Parmesan

Heat the oil in a saucepan and cook the onion for 10 minutes. Add the anchovies, parsley, garlic, celery, rosemary and sage and cook over a low heat for 5 minutes. Add the tomatoes and cook for 30 minutes. Mix the wine, salt and pepper into the sauce and cook for another minute. Taste for seasoning.

Cook the pasta in a large pan of boiling salted water for about 8 minutes, or according to the packet instructions, until *al dente*. Transfer to a serving dish, pour the sauce over the top and sprinkle with grated Parmesan cheese.

Serves 4

kcal 433; kJ 1837; protein 16 (g); fat 6 (g); CHO 78 (g)

Rigatoni with Tuna and Tomato Sauce

1 garlic clove, chopped

200 g (7 oz) can tuna in brine, drained and coarsely flaked

3 tablespoons chopped parsley

2 tablespoons tomato purée

250 ml (8 fl oz) fish stock

500 g (1 lb) dried rigatoni, penne or macaroni

salt and pepper

Heat a large frying pan and dry-fry the garlic for 3–6 minutes, turning constantly, until soft and just beginning to colour. Add the flaked tuna, 2 tablespoons of the parsley, the tomato purée and fish stock. Season to taste with salt and pepper, then simmer gently for 15 minutes.

Meanwhile, bring a large pan of salted water to the boil. Add the pasta, stir and cook for about 10 minutes, or according to the packet instructions, until *al dente*. Drain, mix with the tuna sauce and transfer to a serving dish. Sprinkle with the remaining chopped parsley and serve at once.

Serves 4

kcal 494; kJ 2106; protein 27 (g); fat 3 (g); CHO 97 (g)

Tomato, Anchovy and Olive Sauce

2 teaspoons olive oil

3 garlic cloves, finely
   chopped

1–2 fresh chillies, deseeded and finely
   chopped

50 g (2 oz) anchovy fillets, drained
   and chopped

125 g (4 oz) black olives, pitted and
   chopped

1½ tablespoons capers,
   drained

750 g (1½ lb) tomatoes, skinned and
   chopped

2 tablespoons tomato purée

1 tablespoon chopped basil

3 tablespoons chopped flat leaf
   parsley

500 g (1 lb) spaghetti or linguine

salt and pepper

Heat the oil in a pan and gently fry the garlic, chilli and anchovies until the garlic begins to change colour. Add the olives, capers, tomatoes and tomato purée. Simmer for 30 minutes until thickened. Season to taste with salt and pepper, then add the basil and half of the parsley.

Cook the pasta in plenty of boiling salted water for about 8 minutes, or according to the packet instructions, until *al dente*.

Drain and toss with half of the sauce. Transfer to a serving dish and spoon the remaining sauce over the top. Sprinkle with the remaining parsley and serve immediately.

Serves 6

kcal 360; kJ 1529; protein 14 (g); fat 6 (g); CHO 67 (g)

Shrimp Scampi Pasta

In this interesting Calabrian way of serving pasta, juicy pink prawns are tossed in a lemon and garlic sauce with tender strands of linguine. This dish is very popular among Italian immigrants in the United States.

375 g (12 oz) dried linguine or
   spaghetti
1 teaspoon olive oil
juice of 2 lemons
3 garlic cloves, crushed
150 ml (¼ pint) dry white wine
1 bunch of parsley, finely chopped
500 g (1 lb) raw tiger prawns,
   shelled
sea salt and black pepper

Cook the pasta in a large saucepan of boiling salted water for about 8 minutes, or according to the packet instructions, until the pasta is *al dente*. Drain well.

Meanwhile, heat the olive oil, lemon juice, garlic and white wine in a large, deep frying pan. Heat gently, stirring occasionally, for a few minutes. Add half the parsley and a little salt and pepper and turn up the heat.

Add the shelled prawns and cook for 1–2 minutes, until they turn pink underneath and then turn them over and cook for 1–2 minutes on the other side.

Add the drained linguine or spaghetti to the pan with the remaining parsley and turn the pasta gently in the lemony sauce until all the strands are coated. Serve immediately with a crisp salad tossed with a fat-free dressing.

Serves 4

kcal 400; kJ 1700; protein 22 (g); fat 3 (g); CHO 70 (g)

Conchiglie with Smoked Salmon

To reduce the costs of making this luxurious pasta dish, you could buy smoked salmon offcuts or trimmings which are cheaper than the sliced best smoked salmon. Although you can use black 'caviare' lumpfish roe, the red roe looks much prettier.

375 g (12 oz) dried conchiglie
125 g (4 oz) smoked salmon, cut into
   thin strips
1 teaspoon chopped tarragon
   or dill

300 g (10 oz) very low-fat natural
   fromage frais
25 g (1 oz) drained red caviare
   (lumpfish roe)
salt and pepper

Cook the conchiglie in plenty of boiling lightly salted water for about 10 minutes, or according to the packet instructions, until *al dente*. Drain well in a colander and then transfer to a large warm bowl.

Add the smoked salmon strips and chopped tarragon or dill and stir well to distribute the salmon and herbs evenly through the pasta.

Stir in the fromage frais and season to taste with salt and pepper. Serve the pasta immediately before it cools, sprinkled with red caviare.

Serves 4

kcal 414; kJ 1760; protein 26 (g); fat 4 (g); CHO 75 (g)

far left: tomato, anchovy and olive sauce

Pasta with Tuna Sauce

875 g (1¾ lb) canned tomatoes
1 teaspoon olive oil
2 garlic cloves, each cut into
   3–4 pieces
200 g (7 oz) can tuna in brine,
   drained and flaked
375 g (12 oz) dried pasta of your
   choice
salt and pepper
small bunch of parsley, roughly
   chopped, to garnish

Start making the tuna sauce before cooking the chosen pasta. Crush the tomatoes or blend them briefly in a liquidizer. Heat the oil in a large frying pan until hot, then add the garlic and fry gently until golden. Add the tomatoes, season to taste and simmer gently for about 10–15 minutes. Add the tuna and heat through gently.

Cook the pasta in boiling salted water for about 10 minutes, or according to the packet instructions, until *al dente*. Drain and transfer to a serving dish, then pour over the sauce. Garnish with the parsley.

Serves 4

kcal 412; kJ 1755; protein 25 (g);
fat 3 (g); CHO 76 (g)

left: pasta with tuna sauce
right: penne with Mediterranean fish
sauce

Penne with Mediterranean Fish Sauce

1 small onion, finely chopped
2 garlic cloves, finely chopped
1 small red pepper, cored, deseeded and diced
1 small green pepper, cored, deseeded and diced
425 g (14 oz) can chopped tomatoes

4 tablespoons finely chopped flat leaf parsley
500 g (1 lb) cod fillet, boned, skinned and cubed
500 g (1 lb) dried penne or rigatoni
salt and pepper

Heat a wok and dry-fry the onion, garlic and peppers for 3–6 minutes, turning constantly, until soft. Stir in the tomatoes, parsley and fish, and season to taste. Simmer, uncovered, until the fish is just tender.

Bring a large pan of salted water to the boil. Add the pasta, stir and cook for about 10 minutes, or according to the packet instructions, until *al dente*. Drain and toss with half of the sauce. Transfer to a serving dish. Spoon the remaining sauce over the top and serve immediately.

Serves 6

kcal 376; kJ 1602; protein 26 (g); fat 2 (g); CHO 68 (g)

Tuna Sauce with Tomatoes and Garlic

non-fat spray, for spraying

1 garlic clove, chopped

200 g (7 oz) can tuna in brine, drained and coarsely flaked

3 tablespoons chopped fresh parsley

2 tablespoons tomato purée

250 ml (8 fl oz) fish stock

500 g (1 lb) dried elbow macaroni, rigatoni, or penne

salt and pepper

Spray a pan with non-fat spray and place over a low heat. Add the garlic and cook until beginning to colour. Add the tuna, 2 tablespoons of the parsley, the tomato purée and stock. Season to taste with salt and pepper. Simmer gently for 15 minutes.

Meanwhile, cook the pasta in plenty of boiling salted water for about 10 minutes, until *al dente*.

Drain and mix with the tuna sauce, then transfer to a heated serving dish. Sprinkle with the remaining parsley and serve immediately.

Serves 4

kcal 494; kJ 2105; protein 27 (g); fat 3 (g); CHO 96 (g)

below: *tuna sauce with tomatoes and garlic*
right: *spaghetti with sardines and fennel*

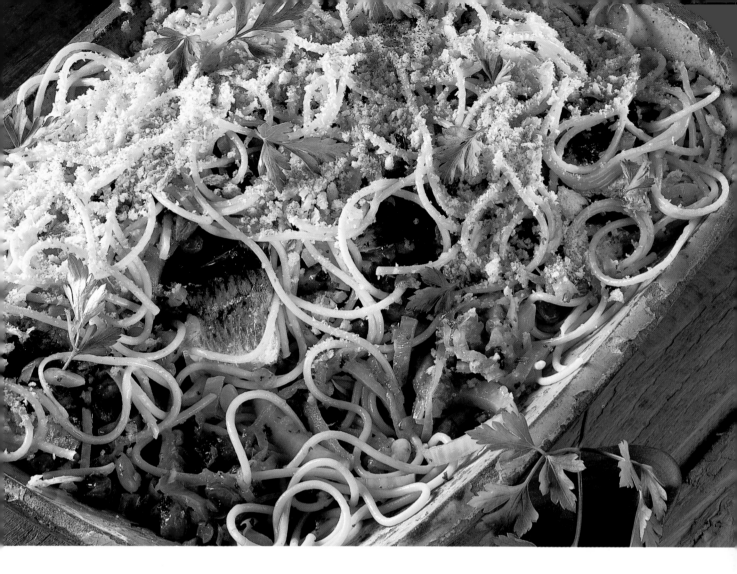

Spaghetti with Sardines and Fennel

1 head fennel, quartered

1 teaspoon olive oil

2 garlic cloves, crushed

250 g (8 oz) fresh sardines, cleaned, trimmed and filleted

non-fat spray, for spraying

2 large onions, thinly sliced

1 tablespoon sultanas

4 anchovy fillets, chopped

2 tablespoons chopped parsley

150 ml (¼ pint) white wine or fish stock

375 g (12 oz) dried spaghetti

lightly browned white breadcrumbs

salt and pepper

Cook the fennel in boiling salted water until almost tender. Drain well, reserving the cooking liquid. Chop the fennel coarsely. Heat the oil in a clean pan and add the garlic. Cook gently until golden brown, then add the sardines and cook gently for 10 minutes.

Meanwhile, spray another pan with non-fat spray and place over a low heat. Cook the onions until they are soft and golden brown. Add the fennel, sultanas, anchovies, parsley and wine or stock. Season lightly with salt and pepper and then cook over a moderate heat for 10 minutes.

Cook the spaghetti in boiling salted water to which the fennel water has been added, for about 8 minutes, or according to the packet instructions, until al dente. Drain well and place half in an ovenproof dish. Cover with half of the sardines and a little of the fennel. Repeat the layers and sprinkle breadcrumbs over the top. Cook in a preheated oven, 180°C (350°F), Gas Mark 4, for 20 minutes.

Serves 4

kcal 517; kJ 2187; protein 27 (g); fat 9 (g); CHO 87 (g)

Casarecchie with Sea Bass

1 teaspoon olive oil

1 garlic clove, finely chopped

½ green pepper, cored, deseeded and
   chopped

1 small onion, finely chopped

250 g (8 oz) can tomatoes

1 tablespoon lemon juice

1 tablespoon chopped basil

4 sea bass fillets, each weighing
   125 g (4 oz) each

300 g (10 oz) dried casarecchie or
   penne

salt and pepper

Heat the oil in a frying pan and add the garlic, green pepper and onion. Stir constantly for about 5 minutes until softened. Add the tomatoes and their juice, lemon juice and basil and cook for a further 5 minutes, breaking up the tomatoes with a wooden spoon.

Arrange the sea bass fillets in a single layer in a shallow baking dish and pour over the sauce. Cover the dish with kitchen foil and place in a preheated oven, 180°C (350°F), Gas Mark 4, and bake for about 15–20 minutes until the fish flakes easily.

Meanwhile, bring a large pan of lightly salted water to the boil. Add the pasta, stir and cook for about 10 minutes, or according to the packet instructions, until *al dente*. Drain the pasta and turn into a warm serving dish. Add the flaked fish and its sauce, toss gently and serve at once.

Serves 4

kcal 411; kJ 1743; protein 34 (g);
fat 5 (g); CHO 60 (g)

below: casarecchie with sea bass
right: tagliatelle with fresh salmon
and dill

Tagliatelle with Fresh Salmon and Dill

200 g (7 oz) salmon fillet

3 tablespoons dry white wine

1 tablespoon chopped dill

no–fat spray, for spraying

4 tablespoons very low-fat natural
  fromage frais

425 g (14 oz) fresh tagliatelle verde

salt and pepper

dill sprigs, to garnish

Remove the skin and bones from the salmon. Slice the flesh thinly and place it in a shallow dish with the wine and dill. Cover and leave for about 20 minutes to marinate, turning occasionally.

Spray a pan with no–fat spray and heat gently. Add the salmon and its marinade and season to taste. Poach gently for 8–10 minutes or until the fish is cooked. Stir in the fromage frais and heat through gently.

Meanwhile, cook the tagliatelle, in salted boiling water for about 3–4 minutes, or according to the packet instructions, until *al dente*.

Drain well and divide the tagliatelle equally between 4 warm soup plates. Pour over the salmon and dill sauce and garnish with dill sprigs. Serve immediately.

Serves 4

kcal 444; kJ 1784; protein 24 (g);
fat 8 (g); CHO 66 (g)

Tagliatelle with Smoked Salmon Sauce

500 g (1 lb) dried tagliatelle

200 ml (7 fl oz) very low-fat natural fromage frais

50 g (2 oz) smoked salmon, cut into thin strips

salt and pepper

1 tablespoon grated Parmesan cheese

Cook the pasta in a large pan of boiling salted water, for about 8 minutes, or according to the packet instructions, until *al dente*. Drain well, reserving a little of the cooking water, then return to the pan and stir in the fromage frais and smoked salmon. Season to taste with salt and plenty of pepper.

Heat through very gently, adding a little of the hot pasta cooking water to moisten it, if wished. Transfer the pasta to a serving dish and gently mix in the Parmesan. Serve immediately.

Serves 4

kcal 486; kJ 2065; protein 23 (g); fat 4 (g); CHO 96 (g)

above: tagliatelle with smoked salmon sauce
right: noodles with fish sauce

Noodles with Fish Sauce

Fresh low-fat noodles have been used in this recipe. These are now available in many supermarkets and specialist food stores. You can buy ready-made fish stock in packets, fresh or frozen, but the dish will have a better flavour if you make the stock yourself by boiling up water with fresh vegetables, fish bones, heads and trimmings, then strain.

10 canned anchovy fillets
2–3 tablespoons skimmed milk
25 g (1 oz) low-fat spread
1 large onion, chopped
2 garlic cloves, thinly sliced
150 ml (¼ pint) dry white wine
250 ml (8 fl oz) fish stock
175 g (6 oz) cooked peeled prawns
2–3 tablespoons chopped parsley
500 g (1 lb) fresh low-fat noodles
salt and pepper
To garnish:
anchovy fillets
whole prawns

Wash the anchovies in water and then pat dry with kitchen paper. Put them into a bowl with the milk and leave to soak for 30 minutes. Drain the anchovies, chop and set aside.

Melt half of the low-fat spread in a saucepan, add the onion and cook for about 10 minutes, stirring, until golden brown. Add the garlic and cook for 1 minute. Add the wine, bring to the boil and cook rapidly until reduced by half.

Add the stock, anchovies, prawns and seasoning and cook, uncovered, for 2 minutes. Remove the pan from the heat and stir in the parsley.

Bring a large saucepan of salted water to the boil. Add the noodles, stir and cook for about 3–4 minutes, or according to the packet instructions, until *al dente*. Drain thoroughly and turn into a warm serving dish. Add the remaining low-fat spread and toss well.

Reheat the sauce for 1 minute and then pour over the noodles and toss well. Serve hot, garnished with anchovy fillets and whole prawns.

Serves 6

kcal 349; kJ 1400; protein 19 (g);
fat 5 (g); CHO 54 (g)

Fusilli
with Mussels

1 kg (2 lb) fresh mussels in their shells

300 ml (½ pint) water

150 ml (¼ pint) dry white wine

1 bouquet garni

375 g (12 oz) dried wholewheat fusilli
  or other pasta shapes

300 ml (½ pint) natural yogurt

2 tablespoons chopped parsley

salt and pepper

lemon balm, to garnish

Thoroughly scrub the mussels in several bowls of clean water and pull off the beards. Tap the mussels and discard any that do not close.

Put them into a large saucepan with the water and wine, bring to the boil, then cover the pan and steam gently for 5–6 minutes, or until the shells have opened.

Drain the mussels and reserve the cooking liquid. Remove the mussels from their shells, leaving about 8 in the shell to use as a garnish. Discard any unopened mussels.

Pour the mussel liquid into a pan, add the bouquet garni, bring to the boil and fast-boil for 10 minutes, or until reduced by two-thirds. Discard the bouquet garni.

Bring a large saucepan of salted water to the boil. Add the pasta, stir and cook for 10–12 minutes, or according to the packet instructions, until *al dente*. Drain, refresh in hot water and then drain again. Put the pasta and mussels into a saucepan and season with pepper. Toss well. Beat the reserved mussel liquid with the yogurt, stir in the parsley and pour over the pasta. Toss well. Turn into a warmed serving dish, garnish with lemon balm and the reserved mussels.

Serves 4

kcal 510; kJ 2170; protein 39 (g); fat 7 (g); CHO 73 (g)

Spaghetti with Mussels and Tomato Sauce

1 kg (2 lb) fresh mussels in their shells
non-fat spray, for spraying
1 onion, chopped
3 garlic cloves, crushed
750 g (1½ lb) tomatoes, skinned and chopped
500 g (1 lb) spaghetti
3 tablespoons chopped parsley
salt and pepper

Put the mussels in a large bowl, cover with cold water and discard any that are open, cracked or rise to the surface. Scrub them well under cold running water to remove any barnacles and the beards.

Place them in a large saucepan with 125 ml (4 fl oz) water, cover and cook over a moderate heat until the mussels open, shaking the pan occasionally. Discard any mussels that do not open. Drain the mussels and remove their shells, leaving a few in their shells for the garnish.

Spray a frying pan with non-fat spray and place over a low heat. Add the onion and garlic and cook gently until golden. Add the tomatoes and season with salt and pepper. Cook gently until the mixture is thickened and reduced.

Stir in the shelled mussels and continue simmering the sauce over a low heat for 2–3 minutes, or until the mussels are heated through.

Meanwhile, cook the pasta in plenty of salted boiling water until *al dente* – 3–4 minutes for fresh or 8 minutes for dried, or according to the packet instructions. Drain well and gently toss with the tomato and mussel sauce. Transfer to a serving dish or 4 warm plates, sprinkle with chopped parsley and garnish with the reserved mussels.

Serves 4

kcal 544; kJ 2314; protein 28 (g); fat 5 (g); CHO 104 (g)

Spaghetti with Baby Clam Sauce

500 g (1 lb) fresh baby clams, in their shells
1 tablespoon olive oil
3 garlic cloves, cut into 3–4 pieces
small bunch of parsley, chopped
375 g (12 oz) dried spaghetti
salt and pepper

Put the clams in a bowl of water and leave for 2–3 hours to allow them to expel any sand in their shells. Wash the clams thoroughly by rubbing the shells together between your hands under running cold water.

Heat the oil in a very large pan and add the garlic. Fry gently until golden, then add the clams and cover the pan. The heat of the oil and the pan will force the clams to open and they will cook in their own juices. Stir occasionally until all of the shells are open. This should take about 10 minutes. The clams will release sea water so it should not be necessary to add salt.

Take half of the clams out of their shells, putting them back in the saucepan and discarding the shells. Add black pepper and chopped parsley. Keep the sauce hot while cooking the spaghetti.

Cook the pasta in plenty of boiling salted water for about 8 minutes, or according to the packet instructions, until *al dente*. Drain well and transfer to a serving dish. Pour the clam sauce over the top and serve.

Serves 4

kcal 369; kJ 1568; protein 16 (g); fat 5 (g); CHO 70 (g)

far left: fusilli twists with mussels

Pappardelle with Seafood Sauce

This delicious mixture of clams, prawns, sole and cod in a fresh tomato sauce is perfect for dinner parties.

1 kg (2 lb) clams, scrubbed

1 tablespoon olive oil

non-fat spray, for spraying

2 onions, finely chopped

250 g (8 oz) plum tomatoes, halved and seeded

250 g (8 oz) cooked peeled prawns

250 g (8 oz) sole fillets, skinned and cut into small pieces

250 g (8 oz) cod fillet, skinned and cut into bite-sized pieces

1 bunch of chives, chopped

375 g (12 oz) fresh pappardelle or fettuccine

salt and pepper

Put the clams in a large shallow pan with the oil. Cover and cook over a high heat for 5–8 minutes until they open. Discard any that do not open. Remove the clams from their shells and put them in a bowl. Strain the cooking liquid through muslin and set aside.

Spray a large pan with non-fat spray and then place over a low heat. Add the onions and cook until golden. Add the strained clam cooking liquid and simmer for 10 minutes, then add the shelled clams and tomatoes. Add the prawns, sole and cod, and simmer gently for 15 minutes, until cooked through. Sprinkle with chives, season to taste and keep hot.

Meanwhile, cook the pasta in plenty of salted boiling water for 3–4 minutes, or according to the packet instructions, until *al dente*. Drain the pasta well, then mix with the seafood sauce and serve immediately.

Serves 6

kcal 400; kJ 1697; protein 39 (g); fat 5 (g); CHO 52 (g)

Pasta with Fisherman's Sauce

425 g (14 oz) can tomatoes

400 g (13 oz) mixed cooked molluscs and shellfish, e.g. prawns, clams, mussels, squid, baby octopus, cuttlefish

1 tablespoon olive oil

2 garlic cloves, crushed

1 fresh red chilli, left whole

375 g (12 oz) dried pasta of your choice

4 tablespoons chopped parsley

salt and pepper

Crush the tomatoes or purée them briefly in a blender or food processor. Peel or shell the shellfish and cut the squid, cuttlefish and octopus into small pieces.

Heat the oil in a large frying pan and add the garlic and chilli. Fry the garlic until golden and crush the chilli against the bottom of the pan to release its flavour. Add the pieces of squid, cuttlefish and octopus to the hot oil and fry, stirring them occasionally, for about 5–6 minutes.

Add the tomatoes and salt and pepper to taste and simmer gently for about 30 minutes, adding the mussels, clams and prawns 10 minutes before the sauce is ready. While cooking, stir the sauce occasionally and add a little water if necessary to prevent it sticking.

Cook the pasta in plenty of boiling salted water, for about 10 minutes, or according to the packet instructions, until *al dente*. Drain well and transfer to a serving dish. Add some of the chopped parsley and pour the hot sauce over the top. Serve garnished with the remaining parsley and a few mussel and clam shells if available.

Serves 4

kcal 454; kJ 1928; protein 28 (g); fat 6 (g); CHO 74 (g)

Spaghetti with Clam Sauce

425 g (14 oz) can tomatoes

4 tablespoons dry red or white wine

2 tablespoons finely chopped parsley

2 teaspoons finely chopped basil

1 small onion, finely chopped

2 garlic cloves, crushed

300 g (10 oz) can baby clams, well drained

300 g (10 oz) dried spaghetti

salt and pepper

chopped parsley, to garnish

Put the canned tomatoes with their juice in a food processor or blender. Add the wine and herbs and blend.

Heat a wok or heavy saucepan and dry-fry the onion for 3–6 minutes, turning constantly. Add the garlic, puréed tomatoes and seasoning. Cover and simmer gently for about 15 minutes, stirring occasionally. Stir the clams into the sauce and heat through.

Meanwhile, bring a large pan of salted water to the boil. Add the spaghetti, stir and cook for about 8 minutes, or according to the packet instructions, until *al dente*. Drain the spaghetti well and turn it into a warmed serving bowl. Pour over the sauce and garnish with chopped parsley. Serve immediately.

Serves 4

kcal 347; kJ 1474; protein 22 (g); fat 2 (g); CHO 61 (g)

above: spaghetti with clam sauce

Spaghetti with Prawn Sauce

1 onion, chopped

2 garlic cloves, crushed

500 g (1 lb) tomatoes, skinned and chopped

½ teaspoon dried basil

375 g (12 oz) cooked peeled prawns

150 ml (¼ pint) white wine

2 tablespoons chopped parsley

500 g (1 lb) dried spaghetti

salt and pepper

Put the onion and garlic into a saucepan with a little water and simmer until soft. Add the tomatoes and basil, season with salt and pepper and simmer for a further 10 minutes. Stir in the prawns, white wine and half of the parsley, then simmer gently for 10 minutes.

Bring a large saucepan of salted water to the boil. Add the pasta, stir and cook for about 8 minutes, or according to the packet instructions, until *al dente*. Drain the pasta and transfer to a warm serving dish. Pour over the prawn sauce, sprinkle with the remaining parsley and serve.

Serves 4

kcal 588; kJ 2497; protein 38 (g); fat 4 (g); CHO 99 (g)

left: spaghetti with prawn sauce
right: farfalle with spinach and prawns

Farfalle with Spinach and Prawns

500 g (1 lb) peeled cooked prawns, defrosted and thoroughly dried if frozen
375 g (12 oz) dried farfalle
250 g (8 oz) spinach leaves, washed and dried and torn into pieces
salt

Marinade:
1 tablespoon coriander seeds
1 tablespoon olive oil
3–4 garlic cloves, crushed
2 tablespoons dry white wine
2 tablespoons Pernod
finely grated rind and juice of 1 lime
salt and pepper

Make the marinade. Dry-fry the coriander seeds in a non-stick frying pan for a few seconds until they give off a spicy aroma. Transfer them to a mortar and crush finely with a pestle. Place in a large bowl with the remaining marinade ingredients. Whisk well to mix.

Add the prawns to the marinade, coating them well. Cover and leave to marinate in the refrigerator or a cold place for about 3–4 hours, stirring occasionally.

Bring a large saucepan of salted water to the boil. Add the pasta, stir and bring back to the boil. Cook for about 8 minutes, or according to the packet instructions, stirring occasionally, until *al dente*. Drain well and turn into a warm bowl. Add the prawns and marinade and toss them together. Add the spinach and toss again. Adjust the seasoning if necessary. Divide the pasta equally between 8 warm soup plates and serve at once.

Serves 8 as a starter

kcal 260; kJ 1106; protein 21 (g); fat 4 (g); CHO 36 (g)

Spaghetti with Shellfish

2 teaspoons olive oil

2 garlic cloves, crushed

50 g (2 oz) can anchovies in oil, drained and dried

3 tablespoons chopped parsley

1 tablespoon chopped dill

1 red pepper, halved lengthways, cored, deseeded and sliced thinly

125 g (4 oz) prepared squid, cut into rings

150 ml (¼ pint) dry white wine

2 pinches of crushed dried chillies

1 large pinch saffron threads

175 g (6 oz) shelled cooked mussels

175 g (6 oz) peeled cooked prawns, defrosted and thoroughly dried if frozen

150 ml (¼ pint) fish stock

4 shelled scallops, diced (including the coral)

375 g (12 oz) dried spaghetti

salt and pepper

To garnish:

Mediterranean prawns

mussels in their shells

1 tablespoon chopped parsley

1 tablespoon chopped dill

Heat the oil in a heavy pan. Add the garlic and cook until golden. Add the anchovies and herbs and stir, pressing the anchovies so that they break and become almost puréed.

Add the red pepper and squid and cook gently for 5 minutes, stirring. Add the wine, chillies, saffron and pepper, then increase the heat and simmer for 10 minutes until reduced to a thick sauce.

Add the mussels, prawns and stock and simmer for 10 minutes until slightly reduced. Stir in the scallops, cover and cook for 5 minutes. Remove from the heat.

Meanwhile, bring a pan of lightly salted water to the boil. Add the pasta and cook for about 8 minutes until *al dente*.

Drain the pasta and transfer to a warm serving bowl. Pour on the sauce and garnish with prawns, mussel shells and chopped herbs.

Serves 4

kcal 543; kJ 2300; protein 42 (g); fat 8 (g); CHO 74 (g)

Pasta with Mushroom and Seafood Sauce

1 tablespoon olive oil

1 garlic clove, crushed

375 g (12 oz) mushrooms, sliced

500 g (1 lb) squid

125 ml (4 fl oz) dry white wine

1 kg (2 lb) fresh mussels in their shells

2 ripe tomatoes, skinned and chopped

500 g (1 lb) cooked peeled prawns

1 tablespoon chopped parsley

375 g (12 oz) dried pasta of your choice

salt and pepper

To make the sauce, heat the oil in a heavy pan over a low heat. Add the garlic and cook until soft but not browned. Add the mushrooms and fry gently until softened.

Prepare the squid by cutting off the tentacles close to the head. Slit open the body bag and pull out the intestines and clear spine. Wash the bag and tentacles well under cold running water and chop finely. Add to the pan with the wine, cover and cook gently for 40 minutes.

Meanwhile, put the mussels in a large bowl, cover them with cold water and discard any that are open, cracked or rise to the top. Scrub well under cold running water to remove any barnacles and the beards.

Boil 1.2 litres (2 pints) water in a pan and add the mussels. Cover and bring back to the boil. Cook until the mussels open. Drain the mussels, discarding any that have not opened. Remove from their shells.

Add the tomatoes to the mushroom mixture. Season and cook for 15 minutes, then add the shelled mussels, prawns and parsley. Stir together for a few minutes.

Cook the pasta in plenty of salted boiling water for about 10 minutes until *al dente*. Drain well and top with the sauce. Serve immediately.

Serves 6

kcal 455; kJ 1926; protein 48 (g); fat 7 (g); CHO 50 (g)

right: spaghetti with shellfish

Sicilian Pasta with Sardines and Garlic

Fresh sardines are really delicious and bear only a passing resemblance to the sardines you buy in cans. If you don't fancy cleaning the sardines yourself, ask your fishmonger to do this for you.

175 g (6 oz) fresh sardines

2 teaspoons olive oil

2 small onions, finely chopped

6 garlic cloves, crushed

250 g (8 oz) ripe tomatoes, skinned, deseeded and roughly chopped

4 canned anchovy fillets in oil, pounded to a purée with oil from the can

6 black olives, pitted

1 tablespoon capers

1 tablespoon chopped basil

300 g (10 oz) dried pasta

salt and pepper

basil leaves, torn, to garnish

Remove the heads and tails from the sardines. Open the fish out gently with your fingers and then carefully remove the bones. (Don't worry if the fish breaks because it will break during cooking anyway.)

Heat the oil in a heavy saucepan. Add the onions and cook gently, stirring frequently, until they are golden – about 10 minutes. Add the sardines and garlic and stir to coat the sardines in the oil and onion. Add all the remaining ingredients, except the pasta. Cover the pan and cook gently for 10-15 minutes.

Meanwhile, bring a large pan of salted water to the boil. Add the pasta, stir and bring back to the boil. Boil, uncovered, for about 10 minutes, or according to the packet instructions, stirring occasionally, until *al dente*.

Drain the pasta well and divide it equally between 4 warmed soup plates. Taste the sauce for seasoning, and adjust if necessary, then pour the hot sauce over the pasta, garnish with basil and serve at once with bread sticks.

Serves 4

kcal 386; kJ 1634; protein 21 (g); fat 9 (g); CHO 60 (g)

Tagliatelle with Squid

375 g (12 oz) squid, cleaned and cut
  into 5 mm (¼ inch) strips

150 ml (¼ pint) dry white wine

1 bouquet garni

1 tablespoon olive oil

1 large onion, chopped

750 g (1½ lb) tomatoes, skinned,
  deseeded and chopped

2 tablespoons basil

1 tablespoon chopped parsley

1–2 garlic cloves, crushed

500 g (1 lb) fresh tagliatelle

salt and pepper

parsley sprigs, to garnish

Place the squid in a shallow pan with the wine and bouquet garni. Bring to the boil, cover and simmer for 2 minutes. Using a slotted spoon, remove the squid and set aside. Discard the bouquet garni and reserve the cooking liquid.

Heat the oil in a pan, add the onion and cook for 5 minutes, without browning. Stir in the tomatoes and herbs and season to taste with salt and pepper. Strain the reserved liquid into the pan, bring to the boil, cover and simmer for 30 minutes. Add the garlic and boil for about 5 minutes until the sauce is reduced and thickened.

Meanwhile cook the tagliatelle in plenty of boiling salted water for 3–4 minutes, or according to the packet instructions, until *al dente*. Drain and place in a warmed serving dish. Add the squid to the sauce, cook gently for 5 minutes, then pour over the hot pasta. Serve immediately, garnished with the parsley sprigs.

Serves 6

kcal 380; kJ 1535; protein 21 (g);
fat 5 (g); CHO 59 (g)

far left: Sicilian pasta with sardines and garlic
above: *tagliatelle with squid*

Fettuccine alla Trota

2 teaspoons olive oil

1 onion, finely chopped

2 garlic cloves, finely chopped

4 smoked trout, boned and flaked

500 g (1 lb) fresh fettuccine

pinch of ground mace

300 ml (½ pint) very low-fat natural
fromage frais

salt and pepper

To garnish:

1 tablespoon chopped parsley

1 teaspoon red lumpfish roe
(optional)

Heat the oil in a pan, add the onion
and garlic and cook until softened,
then add the flaked smoked trout.

Cook the fettuccine in plenty of
boiling salted water for 3–4
minutes, or according to packet
instructions, until *al dente*. Drain
the pasta and add to the trout
mixture.

Season to taste with salt and
pepper and mace and stir in the
fromage frais. Toss together gently
over a low heat for 1 minute to heat
through and serve garnished with
chopped parsley and red lumpfish
roe, if using.

Serves 4

kcal 579; kJ 2337; protein 42 (g);
fat 8 (g); CHO 84 (g)

Fusilli with Broccoli

375 g (12 oz) dried fusilli
500g (1 lb) broccoli, broken into
   florets
1 teaspoon olive oil
1 small onion, finely chopped
25 g (1 oz) walnuts, roughly chopped
25 g (1 oz) anchovy fillets, chopped
1 tablespoon chopped fresh parsley
salt and pepper

Cook the pasta in plenty of boiling salted water for about 10 minutes, or according to the packet instructions, until *al dente*. Drain and keep warm.

Meanwhile, blanch the broccoli in boiling salted water for 5 minutes. Drain and plunge into cold water immediately to prevent further cooking. Drain again.

Heat the oil in a pan and fry the onion over a low heat for about 10 minutes, stirring occasionally. Stir in the walnuts, anchovies and broccoli and cook slowly over a gentle heat for 3–4 minutes.

Stir in the drained pasta and heat through. Remove from the heat, then add the parsley, season well with pepper and serve immediately.

Serves 4

kcal 414; kJ 1750; protein 19 (g);
fat 9 (g); CHO 69 (g)

Asparagus and Crab Tagliatelle

Both asparagus and crab are in season during the summer, and are at their cheapest and most plentiful. This delicious quick pasta recipe combines them both.

1 teaspoon olive oil
125 g (4 oz) button mushrooms,
   sliced
150 ml (¼ pint) dry white wine
juice of ½ lemon
175 g (6 oz) white crab meat
500 g (1 lb) asparagus, trimmed and
   cut into 2.5 cm (1 inch) lengths
250 g (8 oz) dried tagliatelle
2–3 tablespoons very low-fat natural
   fromage frais (optional)
2 tablespoons finely chopped fresh
   parsley, to garnish
salt and pepper

Heat the olive oil in a frying pan and sauté the mushrooms for 2–3 minutes, turning them frequently, until golden brown. Add the white wine and lemon juice and turn up the heat. Cook vigorously for 4–5 minutes until the liquid has reduced by at least half. Stir in the crab meat and seasoning to taste.

Cook the asparagus in a pan of lightly salted boiling water for 5 minutes until tender. Drain and add to the crab and mushroom sauce.

Meanwhile, cook the tagliatelle in a large pan of lightly salted boiling water for about 8 minutes, or according to the packet instructions, until *al dente*. Drain and toss with the crab meat sauce. If wished, add a little fromage frais for a more creamy texture. Pile the pasta into a large serving dish and sprinkle with chopped parsley. Serve at once.

Serves 4

kcal 378; kJ 1580; protein 23 (g);
fat 7 (g); CHO 51 (g)

far left: fettuccine alla trota

Index